RUNNING WITH YOUR DOG

by
John A. Sanford

Illustrated by
Edgar L. "Ted" Sanford

Edited by
William W. Denlinger and R. Annabel Rathman

Cover Design by
Bob Groves

DENLINGER'S PUBLISHERS, LTD.
Box 76, Fairfax, Virginia 22030

Library of Congress Cataloging-in-Publication Data

Sanford, John A.
    Running with your dog.

    Bibliography: p.
    1. Dogs.   2.Exercise for pets.   3. Running.
I. Denlinger, William Watson.   II. Rathman,
R. Annabel.   III. Title.
SF427.45.S36   1987   636.7'008'33   87-534
ISBN 0-87714-125-8

International Standard Book Number: 0-87714-125-8

DEDICATION
To my family, who often had to wait patiently for me to
return from a run with wet, muddy, happy dogs before we
could eat dinner, and to my great running dogs Doc and
Cori.

Contents

Acknowledgments

My great thanks to Joy Halverson, D.V.M., and Nancy Bickerton, professional dog trainer and breeder, who read this manuscript and offered helpful comments; also to Stewart Dadmun, M.D., and Paul H. Broadley, M.D., who offered sound advice about running. My thanks, too, to Helen Macey for her invaluable help in preparing the manuscript. I am indebted to all these people for their assistance, but if this book contains any mistakes, they are mine.

Introduction

Nearly twenty million people in the United States run regularly, and maybe half of these people own dogs. This book is written to those who run with their dogs and to those who might—if they knew how healthy and enjoyable it could be for them and their canine companions.

There are good books on running and good books on owning a dog, but as far as I know there isn't anything written on running *with* your dog. (One useful but incomplete pamphlet, written and privately published by a veterinarian who runs, is listed at the back of this book in the bibliography.) Apparently the people who write books on dogs are not runners and the people who write books on running are not dog owners, so it hasn't occurred to any of these writers that it would be helpful if they devoted a section of their books to running with your dog as a companion.

This book hopes to fill that gap. It is meant for people who already run with their dogs and want to know more about it, for people who have tried running with their dogs but have encountered problems, and for people who might try it if they had a little guidance and inspiration. It's also written for dog owners who have never run before, but who might like to try it as a form of exercise good for themselves and their four-legged friends.

A word about the organization of this book: The first chapter deals with the unsolved question of how man and dog first struck up their relationship and why it's natural for them to run together. The second chapter is written for people who have not run before but want to know something about it; experienced runners might wish to skip this and go directly to the third chapter, which asks, "Why run with your dog?" The next five chapters are practical and informative, answering your questions about running with a dog and providing other information you might never have thought to ask about.

Most of my information for this book comes from almost twenty years of running thirty to forty-five miles a week with a variety of canine companions. I'm also indebted to the many people I saw running with their dogs and whom I stopped to ask for an interview. Without exception, each was interested and helpful. And I want to thank their dogs, who waited with remarkable patience while I interviewed their masters. (I think they knew we were talking about them.)

When writing a book nowadays, you have to be careful about using the pronoun "he" when referring to persons of both sexes. The statement, "When a person runs with his dog he needs to know how far his dog can run," may read well enough, but if the reader is a woman she might feel left out. On the other hand, using "she" instead of "he" might make some men feel excluded. You could say "he or she" and nobody would be omitted, but you'd be bending the English language into pretzels. My solution is to alternate the use of "he" and "she." I haven't counted which I've used most, but I tried to make it about fifty-fifty.

When it comes to dogs, the situation is even more complicated. Strictly speaking, "dog" refers to the male while "bitch" is the proper term for the female. However, it's too laborious to observe this distinction. So when I use "dog" I mean either a male or female except in special contexts, such as a *dog* being aroused by a *bitch* in heat. As far as I know, the feminist movement hasn't hit our canine companions, and none of the bitches I've met have objected to the common use of dog for both sexes. I hope their owners will be equally agreeable.

How Did It All Start?

Among the predators that inhabited our planet thousands of years ago were human beings and the Canidae family of animals—a family that included wolves, coyotes, jackals, and foxes, to mention just a few of its thirty-nine species. Some of these canids and human beings struck up a relationship and decided to go it together through this world. No one knows just when this first happened—certainly as far back as ten thousand years and probably much longer—but we do know that the many different breeds of the modern dog are descended from those first wild canids that decided it was better to share the campfire with human beings than tough it out alone.

Bones and relics from archaeological digs reveal that people in all parts of the world had dogs as companions. In the ancient Near East, dogs were bred to help in the hunt. The Romans had them in their armies, and the Chinese used them for guard dogs. Europeans became perhaps the greatest breeders of dogs, and most of our contemporary breeds are the results of the efforts by Europeans who wanted a particular kind of dog for a particular purpose. But when Europeans explored Asia, they found dogs there, too. And when they came to North America, they found dogs guarding Indian villages and pulling Indian *travois*.

We don't know how long ago dogs and people first became companions; neither do we know how it happened. Some speculate that wild canids discovered it was easier to hang around the camps of human beings and live from the remains of their kills than to do their own hunting and killing. This unappealing notion is one of many competing theories that try to explain how people and dogs first got together. Being a hopeless romantic, I prefer two other theories, and their supporting evidence explains why some of us run with our dogs today. They are based on the premise that there are two important qualities that canids and human beings share, and that the association between the two species developed because of these common qualities.

The first common trait is the pack instinct. Human beings live in groups. This is partly because we depend on each other for survival and partly because of a matter of preference. We live in clusters—couples, families, villages, cities, nations—and we have strong feelings about "our" group. We are loyal to the members of *our* family, we cheer for *our* school's football team, and we have patriotic feelings for *our* country. People also make close and enduring personal relationships. We make lasting friendships and develop permanent relationships with members of the opposite sex. This bonding between and among people is perhaps our most commendable human characteristic. True, some people are loners, living without friends and apart from others, but we usually look on these people as alienated and strange, a departure from the healthy norm.

We also hurt and destroy each other, which is one of the most disagreeable traits of human nature. That puts us morally a step behind other forms of animal life, which rarely kill a member of their own species.

While certain other animals also live in groups and occasionally show traits of what might be called bonding or affection for each other, none begins to rival our capacity for group living and enduring relationships, except for canids. Most animal unions are transitory, impersonal, and only serve the purpose of procreation. The male bear, for example, mates with the female in early summer but then wanders away to resume his solitary life, leaving her to raise the cubs alone. Hoofed animals, such as elk, antelope, bison, wildebeests, and zebras, live closely together for the purpose of mutual protection, but there is little indication that anything resembling affection develops among them. Canids, however, approximate the capacity of human beings for forming closely knit groups and for establishing lasting personal attachments, and they do not have the disagreeable human trait of killing members of their own species. For, while canids occasionally fight each other to establish dominance or to drive rivals away from their territory, they seldom fight to the death and never kill each other for the sake of killing.

Wolves are the best example of the pack instinct among canids. A pack may include eight to twenty wolves with one dominant wolf who is the leader. Known as the "alpha" wolf, the leader is usually, but not always, a male. The proper place of each individual in the pack is carefully established and maintained. The pack forms a hunting and living unit that endures for years. Members of the pack support each other, play among themselves, and care for all the young. Each pack has its own territory. Should a wolf from another pack intrude, there may be a fight—seldom to the death—until the intruder is driven away. Occasionally, a stray wolf may be taken into the pack after its proper social position has been determined.

Farley Mowat, in his beautiful book *Never Cry Wolf,* tells a story that illustrates the mutual supportiveness of wolves—how the mother wolf gets to run with the pack. Wolves mate for life. When the female wolf is ready to deliver her pups she finds or digs an appropriate hole, gives birth to them, and carefully nourishes and guards them. When the pack makes a kill, they bring back a portion of the meat for the mother wolf and, when the pups are able to eat meat, for the young ones as well. But the mother wolf, it seems, doesn't like being confined just to caring for the young. She'd like to be herself now and then. There is always a single wolf or two hanging around the pack, a male that lost his mate, an unattached female, or an "Uncle Albert" wolf who happens to be a bachelor. From time to time, Mowat observed, one of the unattached wolves remains home with the pups, and mother wolf gets to run with the pack that night.

Coyotes don't form packs like wolves, but they do live in closely knit family units. Perhaps they don't need packs because their food consists of smaller animals, or even berries and fruit—in fact, practically anything, while wolves prefer large game that requires the cooperation of a number of animals for successful hunting. Just the same, coyotes don't like to live alone either. They live in families that may include a mother and a father, the young coyotes, half-grown teenagers, and other adults with a kin relationship.

Hope Ryden, who spent many years studying the habits of coyotes, tells about their affection for each other in her book *God's Dog*. For instance, when the male and female coyote meet again after a time of separation, they nuzzle and lick each other enthusiastically, evidently expressing joy at their reunion. The pups are cared for sternly but fondly by mother and father alike. The pups romp and play freely with each other, then fall asleep in a heap, warmed by each others' bodies.

Wolves also form close personal attachments. When I was a boy I read all the stories of animal life I could find, but the one I loved most was Ernest Thompson Seton's *Wild Animals I Have Known*. My favorite story was "Lobo, King of the Currampaw." Again and again I read the tale of gallant Lobo, the great and canny wolf that no one could shoot, trap, or poison, who was finally brought to his death by his love for his mate, Blanca.

Hired to kill the great Lobo, Seton succeeded no better than his predecessors, but he did succeed in killing Blanca. Instead of disposing of her body, he dragged the dead Blanca over a complex network of strong steel traps, covering the traps with her scent. The desperate Lobo, searching for his mate, lost his usual sense of caution when he came across her scent, and fell into the traps. He was not killed at once but was made a prisoner. Once he realized his hopeless captivity, the great wolf became quiet, seeming to accept his imprisonment without complaint. But one day, when Seton went out to inspect his captive, Lobo was dead. The stress of captivity did what the hardships of a free life couldn't, and evidently Lobo preferred to join Blanca in death rather than cling to a life that had lost its meaning. As for Ernest Thompson Seton, I must confess that I never forgave him for the treacherous deception he used to capture the faithful Lobo.

Of course it is not supposed to be scientific to read human emotions into animal behavior, but nothing could have persuaded me as a boy that Lobo and Blanca were not deeply attached to each other with bonds of affection. The fact is that canids act for all the world as though they like each other, and there is no denying that they do make lasting and loyal relationships. What is important for us is that they are capable of transferring this capacity for both pack living and personal attachments to human beings, the one other animal that matches their capacity for affection and group life.

Legend and fiction have long recognized the capacity of man and wolf to befriend each other. The Romans, for instance, told the story of the she-wolf who adopted the abandoned twins, Romulus and Remus. When the children grew up, they founded the city that took its name from them—Rome. Rudyard Kipling, in his famous *The Jungle Book*, tells of Mowgli, the abandoned waif who was adopted and raised by wolves and then went on to become their leader and save them from the terrible tiger, Shere Khan.

All of this is legend or fiction, but there is at least one true story of a friendship that developed in the wild between a man and a wolf. Robert F. Leslie's book *In the Shadow of a Rainbow* tells the remarkable story of Gregory Tah-Kloma, a Chimmesyan Indian of British Columbia, who in 1964 befriended a 150-pound gray she-wolf.

While this may seem incredible to those of us who were taught to believe that wolves are beasts that devour human beings on sight, Farley Mowat, in the book already mentioned, tells much the same story as Greg. By accident he stumbled on a wolf pack and den. To his surprise he found that his presence didn't seem to bother them very much, so he decided to camp only a few hundred feet away. One day, following the wolves' example, he marked out the boundaries of his camp by urinating at various spots around it. (He says he had to drink vast quantities of tea to accomplish this!) The wolves seemed surprised at his actions, but when Mowat saw the alpha wolf urinating opposite the places where he had placed his "sign," he knew that boundaries between him and the wolves had been successfully established and would be meticulously observed.

Back to Greg, who had been camping alone in the Canadian wilderness when he realized that the place he wanted for a campsite was only a short distance from the home of a wolf pack led by a giant female wolf. Instead of running away or shooting at the wolves, Greg decided to stay where he was and see what would happen. For many days he lived by the wolves and showed by his unobtrusive behavior that he respected their prior right to be there. He then found that he could approach the wolves more closely when he walked about on all fours instead of upright. As long as he did this the wolves showed no nervousness about his presence, and in time they came to ignore him even when he ventured quite close. Evidently they sensed they had no cause to fear him, and so a reserved yet amiable relationship was established.

Greg found that, while most of the wolves ignored him, the alpha wolf—the large female whom he named Náhani—began to show an interest in him. Náhani approached his camp one evening as he sat quietly by his small fire. She sat in the shadows not far away and looked at him intently for hours. She did this for several evenings, sitting a little closer each night. Greg showed no fear. Then one evening the great wolf made physical contact with the Indian. Author Leslie tells the story:

Greg tingled and shivered from head to foot—his teeth chattered, his hands shook—when the long-legged queen wolf stepped slowly out of the darkness and strode deliberately into the circle of campfire light. She sniffed the sweat-laden air, walked to the opposite end of the log, faced the crackling flames, and haunched. Small campfires have always fascinated wolves, and outdoorsmen have often misinterpreted lupine curiosity for aggression. Except for deeply rhythmic breathing, she sat as motionless as a mounted museum specimen.

There is no doubt that something clicked between that wolf and Gregory Tah-Kloma when their eyes finally met. He wanted to believe objectively, without any aura of mystery, that two beings sensed an attraction, one for the other, and at that moment an irresistible friendship began. As an unmated female—as monarch of her pack—Náhani, he felt, was an entity apart from her kind, aloof, alone, and lonely.

Each time their eyes met, further understanding seemed to grow; a bond, shaky and untenable at first, began to bridge the communication chasm between man and wolf. For all her arrogance—no doubt a vital necessity for the queen of a realm—she seemed unable to conceal from Greg an intelligent animal's need for genuine affection. Perhaps Greg was also unable to conceal the same thing from her.*

*Robert Franklin Leslie, *In the Shadow of a Rainbow.* (New York. W. W. Norton and Co., Inc., 1974) pp. 24-25.

The story of how Greg deepened his friendship with Náhani and the wolves, how Náhani saved his life, and how Greg saved the pack from bounty hunters, makes for fascinating reading, but would lead us beyond the scope of this book.

The canid and human capacity for affection and relationship is the psychological foundation of the two species' ability to live together. Maybe the original canids did throw in their lot with humans because they liked to munch away on leftovers. But without their common pack instinct these early canids would have remained thieves and scavengers lurking in the shadows.

The domesticated dog has the same capacity for affection and group living as his primordial ancestors but transfers this instinct to the humans with whom he lives and who now constitute his "pack." And many people value their dog's capacity to give and respond to affection.

Sometimes this pack instinct can be a bit embarrassing. My dog Doc, half Labrador Retriever, half German Shorthaired Pointer, of whom you will hear more as this book progresses, had a particularly strong feeling for his pack of human beings. For many years, at least once during the summer, I would organize a hike into the Sierra Nevada with five or six friends and family members. Naturally Doc would go along. It didn't take Doc long to decide that all the hikers were part of his pack. Even if some were originally strangers to him, he would soon adopt them and include them in his circle of persons who belonged together. Doc would get upset when someone wandered away from the group, and occasionally this was a problem. If, for instance, you wandered from the campsite to take care of the urges of nature, Doc would follow and sit staring intently. Once you finished, he would solemnly escort you back to camp where the rest of the "pack" was waiting.

The fact that both canids and humans share a common instinct to live in closely knit groups and establish ties of personal affection may partly account for the ancient association between the two species. But the second trait the two species share in common is just as important: both canids and humans are excellent runners. In fact, with the possible exception of the horse and caribou, no other animal can match a man, dog, wolf, or coyote when it comes to long distance running. The cheetah is faster over a short distance, as are certain other animals such as bears and ostriches, but none has the combination of speed and endurance that belongs to a healthy and well-conditioned human being or canid.

The human race in general has become so sedentary that many people can't run to the end of the block. Those who exercise regularly know that, with a certain amount of natural disposition and proper conditioning, a human being can run incredibly long distances. Men and women, young and as old as sixty years or more, have trained themselves to run the 26.2-mile marathon. As though this isn't far enough, some runners today compete in fifty-mile races, and several even run the John Muir trail in the Sierra Nevada of California. What's more important, people with only average gifts for running have found they can easily do five, ten, or fifteeen miles at a time.

While we run for pleasure or health, primitive man sometimes had to run for necessity. A good deal of evidence suggests that ancient hunters used to kill their prey by running it to exhaustion. Weapons such as stones or sharpened sticks were only effective at close range and against a relatively helpless prey. A swift and elusive animal had to be run into the ground. Such ancient hunts must have taken place over long distances, ending when the hunter had outrun the prey.

According to Dr. Walter Bortz in an article in *Runner's World* magazine (June 1982) entitled "Primitive Man and Athletics," anatomists have learned that primitive man had a thicker bone structure than does contemporary man. They theorize that this is because primitive man was more physically active. It is a fact that one benefit from exercise is increased bone mass and strength.

Even today, surviving primitive people live a physically active life and hunt by running down their prey. Bortz cites the example of the African Bushmen who get more than one-third of their food supply by chasing and catching game. There are many examples, he tells us, of Bushmen running down large game and killing them when they are exhausted.

Another contemporary people who are prodigious runners are the Tarahumara Indians of the Sierra Madre in northern Mexico. Many observers have reported these Indians' remarkable accomplishment as runners. In his book *Indian Running,* Peter Nabokov tells about their incredible running game: the Indians kick a ball of madrone wood for several days at a time without apparent signs of fatigue. According to Nabokov, as early as 1894 one chronicler told of Tarahumaras who would run 170 miles without stopping, and they were often hired by the Mexicans to round up wild horses. In 1924 Ernest Thompson Seton described a Tarahumaran postman who regularly covered seventy miles a day, seven days a week, carrying his heavy bag of mail. A more contemporary observer, Michael Jenkinson, tells of a Tarahumaran courier he knew who, in 1971, covered fifty miles in six hours with no stops enroute. The women are also prodigious runners; they play a running game with a rolling hoop that is as demanding as the game the men play with the madrone wood ball.

It still is nothing for these Indians to run down a deer, and they still often hunt in this manner. Indeed, tales of American Indians hunting deer in this way are commonplace. It was clearly the accepted hunting technique, especially, as Bortz observes, when the bow and arrow and the horse were not available.

My suggestion is that, in addition to their common instinct for bonding, what originally brought humans and canids together was their ability to run together and their common method of killing prey by running them down. Sometime, many thousands of years ago, the two species found they fared better when they hunted together. The canid had a superior sense of smell, which enabled him to find and track game that people could not see; he could also close in on and kill a good many animals. People had superior intelligence, crude weapons, and the advantage of being taller, so they could see over bushes and for longer

distances. Together they must have made an especially effective hunting unit. This theory can't be proved, of course, but it's just as likely to be correct as any other I know.

The objection might be raised that it is unlikely two species as hostile toward each other as humans and canids would ever have gotten together, the story of Greg and Náhani notwithstanding. Don't people hate and kill wolves? Don't coyotes shun people who try to trap and poison them? Don't foxes live a furtive nocturnal life for fear of people? How could these ancient enemies have ever gotten together?

The interesting fact is that the hostility between human beings and animals is the result of recent centuries, when people tried to exterminate wild animals in general and predators in particular. American Indian observers tell us that in the old days animals weren't wild. They wouldn't automatically run from people, because they knew they had nothing to fear from them. But those were the days when people killed only to eat, and there would have been no reason to kill a wolf or coyote when a deer or bison would make a better meal. Canids, of course, never saw human beings as suitable prey.

Given the natural tendency of humans and canids to bond to each other, plus their ancient affinity for running together, it's natural for men and women today to run with dogs as companions. As we will see later, the natural running relationship between human beings and dogs still exists. But first a word about running for those people who aren't runners now but are intrigued by the idea.

2. You As a Runner

In the movie *Chariots of Fire,* Olympic runner Eric Liddell says, "God made me fast, and it pleasures Him when I run." God didn't make all of us fast, but most of us are able to run, and when we do, it is enjoyable. Joy comes when something performs the function it was created to perform. The body was designed for active use, and when we bring the body into good condition and exercise it, there can be great pleasure in its use.

Running is something we can do at almost any age as long as our health is good. We can run alone, with a companion, in a group, and both men and women can run. We can run any time of the day, in almost any weather, and it will cost us almost nothing.

THE PHYSICAL BENEFITS OF RUNNING

The adage, "if you don't use it, you will lose it," is certainly true of the body. It has all kinds of abilities, but if we don't use them, we will lose them. When muscles aren't used, they atrophy. When a leg is immobilized in a cast, it shrinks. When the heart isn't made to pump hard occasionally, it gets weak and the arteries begin to clog up. The body is self-renewing. The more it is used the stronger and better it gets—up to a point.

When you run you use your cardiovascular system, lungs, and most of the muscles in your lower torso. Running strengthens the heart. It becomes more efficient, and your pulse gets slower as you get in better condition. When you first start running, your resting pulse might be 80; when you are in good shape, it may have dropped to 60 or 55 or even 50. If you have a tendency to high blood pressure, running may help keep it down; if you don't, running may keep it normal. What is less well known is that running and other forms of exercise prevent osteoporosis. Osteoporosis is a disease of the bones that sometimes comes to people later in life, especially women. Bones lose mass, and are deprived of calcium, consequently they break with the slightest fall. Research shows that the more bones are used the more they build up mass and strength and retain calcium. Osteoporosis is a "disease of civilization," an ailment that comes when we no longer use our bodies the way they were meant to be used.

Running burns calories faster than any other form of exercise. People who run are aware of how warm they get—even in quite crisp weather you can stay warm when you run briskly enough. That warmth is an indication of the calories your body is consuming, and this makes running especially beneficial for weight loss and weight control. Running also decreases rather than increases the appetite. After a hard run you might think you would be ravenous, but, according to current theory, fatty acids have accumulated in the blood that prevent a "hunger signal" from going to the brain. You will eventually feel hungry, but only for what your body actually needs.

When you run you burn excess fat; even better, you are probably burning the sickest cells in your body. One theory about the benefit of occasional fasting is that when the body begins to use its reserves for fuel it starts by consuming the weakest cells, leaving the healthiest. The same thing probably takes place in long-distance running.

Running helps you stop smoking—and keep off the cigarettes after you have stopped. Very few people remain smokers once they start running, and when they stay on cigarettes, they smoke much less than they did before. This is partly because the psychological need for cigarettes is diminished, and partly because the negative effects of smoking on breathing and general well-being show up so markedly when you run that it's a lot easier to get motivated to stop.

Of course, running isn't for everyone, and it doesn't do everything for you. Some people like to run. Their bodies enjoy it, and their souls enjoy it too. Other people say they get bored running, and others may not be physically suited for the exercise. If you don't like running for one reason or another, you certainly are not likely to do it for long, but don't feel bad or guilty; just find another form of exercise that you do like. Swimming is first-rate exercise. It has many of the physical benefits of running with less danger of injury. The trouble is you have to have a pool and may be restricted to the warm seasons. The sport of trampolining will provide good exercise for you too. Biking is also first-rate exercise, except, most of us have to look out for traffic, which keeps it from being the meditative experience some people find in running. Tennis, racquetball, and gardening are all beneficial, and some may help upper torso development too, which running usually doesn't do. When all else fails, walk. In fact, good brisk walking, the kind that gets your heart pumping hard, greatly benefits everyone and is suited for people of all physical types and dispositions. There *is* a form of exercise for you, and if it isn't running it may be walking. Incidentally, your dog will enjoy walks with you almost as much as runs, and many statements in this book about running with your dog also apply to walking with your dog.

THE PSYCHOLOGICAL BENEFITS OF RUNNING

The psychological and spiritual benefits of running are less well known than the physical benefits. For many people running is a way to get back into oneself. I remember having a brief talk with a harassed young executive just before he set out on his run. As he began I called to him, "Well, they can't get to you out here." And it's true. Out on his run, the young man was alone with himself, his soul, and his thoughts. Running is a time for reflection, for "processing" all the many thoughts, wounds, and experiences that have come to us during the day. It's a time when many people get the influences of other people out of their system and get back into their own soul and body. For them it isn't just physical exercise, it's spiritual exercise, a way of meditating, of making the conscious mind open to all kinds of thoughts, fantasies, and creative urges that ordinarily are shoved aside in the hurly-burly of a busy, extraverted life.

Running is a natural antidote to depression. In fact, some psychiatrists prescribe it for their depressed patients. There are several reasons for this. First, depression is characterized by shallow breathing. Running, or any other aerobic form of exercise, requires deep breathing—and this in itself relieves depression. It doesn't, of course, cure underlying psychological problems that may be behind the depression. But when it works, running is a healthier anti-depressant than drugs with their negative side effects. It helps us sleep more readily and deeply, and it helps us require less sleep for optimal functioning.

There's also a theory that running elevates our mood because it causes the brain to manufacture more endorphins, the natural chemicals produced when we are in pain or under stress. The endorphins produced during running can alter the depressed state that often results from the difficulties and frustrations of daily life.

Running also tends to relieve depression because we begin to feel physically and mentally so much better. A sluggish body produces a sluggish mind prone to depression. The increased vitality of a body that is healthy and in good condition helps to renew the soul.

Running builds confidence. A friend took up running at age sixty-five. It was hard going at first, but he gradually worked up to two miles. One day he came in and reported that he had run clear out to the end of a certain road—three miles! "I feel like a hero," he commented. And he was a hero. He put himself to the test and reached a goal; he drove his body even when it hurt and did something he had never done before. When people run, everybody's a winner and everyone's a bit of a hero.

Naturally, when running works well for someone in the ways I've suggested, that person wants to run again—and again and again. It is said that some people become addicted to running and like any addiction, matters can go too far. People may try to solve problems by running that should be solved in another way. But there's also evidence that everyone must get addicted to something. There's always going to be something in life that we turn to consciously or unconsciously to help us keep going. Many of the things we turn to are destructive. When we become addicted to alcohol, drugs, or overeating, we have a "negative addiction." If we must become addicted to something, better that it be a "positive addiction," something that makes us healthy instead of sick. So if you think you might get addicted to running, don't worry. As long as it doesn't go too far, it may help you avoid negative addictions.

Finally, running can help you develop relationships. Many people find congenial companionship in this way. Some have a "running buddy" or two, and others run with a group. And, as I have said, some people prefer to run alone so they can have time with their own thoughts. If you want the best of both worlds, you will run with your dog. As we will see, your dog may be the ideal running companion. He will not interrupt your thoughts but will be a constant and affectionate buddy with whom you can share the pleasures of your run.

Let's assume you've never run before and want to start. Here are suggestions on how to begin.

First, you have to ask how healthy you are. I've stressed the physical benefits of running, but you need to know from where you're starting. If your body is free of disease, a proper running program can increase your health and vitality. However, if you have a health problem, you need to be careful; in fact, running may not be for you at all. Therefore, the place to begin may be a trip to your doctor for an examination. If you decide you want to run, tell your doctor. It's best to have a personal physician for this purpose—someone who really knows you and whom you can trust. Others things being equal, it's also best to go to a doctor who is a runner. Doctors who don't run may have a prejudice against it; doctors who do will want to encourage you as much as they can.

Your doctor may want to give you an Exercise Heart Test. This test puts your heart under increasing physical stress while the doctor or a technician carefully monitors its performance. The test checks for any malfunctioning that may show up only when the heart is working extra hard. If there is a problem, it doesn't necessarily mean you can't run. A properly supervised running program actually alleviates certain heart problems. However, safety requires proper medical supervision.

Let's assume that you are basically healthy enough to undertake a program of sustained and increasingly vigorous exercise. You're ready to go, and although you may not know it, your body is eager also. It *wants* to get into optimum shape. Remember, your body is much stronger, has far more endurance, and is capable of much more than you realize. It is a marvelous organism, the product of hundreds of thousands of years of Mother Nature's best efforts. It's capable of giving its best again and again and liking it.

At first you may feel as though you can't even run to the end of the block. If you can't, don't be discouraged. Run as far as you comfortably can—then run a little farther until it hurts a bit, until your heart is working, and your breath is running short. Then stop. That's far enough for a first experience. How far did you go? Half a block? A quarter of a mile? It doesn't really matter; what does is that the next time you will run a little bit farther. Chances are this won't be difficult. You have asked your body to run a certain distance and it has. In doing so, it has become stronger. Everything in you works a bit better now. Your heart now pumps a little more efficiently, your blood cells deliver their oxygen to your muscles a little better, your lungs are a little more elastic, and your legs are stronger. If you ran half a block before, now you may find you can go three-quarters of a block, and that quarter of a mile has become a third of a mile. Do this for two or three weeks, and you'll be surprised how far you can go. The distance you could barely run when you first started is now just a warmup for you.

It's not all downhill though. One day you may start to run and feel "flat." Your body feels listless. The distance you ran so easily yesterday is a chore today. You feel discouraged. Don't be—just take a day or two off. Training the body is a matter of pushing it close to its limit, then backing off and letting it rebuild. Using the body makes it stronger, but it also uses up vital body elements. Muscles get tiny tears in them; muscle cells get depleted of glycogen and need time to "refuel," and essential electrolytes are consumed that have to be replaced. "Waste" materials develop when your body consumes energy fast, and the body needs time to expel them. So when you feel "flat," let your body rest or engage in an alternate, lighter exercise for a day or so, then get back to your running. Chances are when you return after your rest you'll feel stronger than ever.

If you miss a day or two of running, you won't lose your carefully built up conditioning. You might if you miss a week or two, but a short time may actually help you. Athletes competing in running events never run right up to the time of the event; if they did they would leave their best race on the training track. Several days, or maybe even a week before the race, they stop training or slow up drastically, so they will be at their physical optimum at the time of the race.

When you first begin to run, you may also want to "run-walk." Run about as far as you can, stop and walk about half the distance you ran, then run again. Keep this up as long as you can. It will help you increase your distance more rapidly.

After you have built up your distance to a certain length—let's say you're now running a mile or two, maybe three—learn to do "wind sprints," at first at the end of your run and then during your run. As you near the place where you're going to stop, run the last hundred yards or quarter of a mile at a brisker pace. Feel your heart speed up and your breathing get deeper. This will build up your wind. Remember, your wind development will only increase as you place greater demands on it. At first it may hurt a bit as you pull in all that air, but you will soon find that it gets easier to run faster, and with that comes a feeling of greater confidence in yourself. Later you may wish to incorporate bursts of faster running into your total running experience by now and then altering your pace, speeding up for a short while, then slowing down again to your regular speed.

How far should you run? That's up to you—and your body, your disposition, and your needs. There is some evidence that the optimum physical benefits are reached when you run three or four times a week for a total of perhaps fifteen miles. However, some of the psychological benefits I have described are often only achieved after longer runs. Anything farther than fifteen miles may be enjoyable and psychologically beneficial but not necessarily more physically beneficial than when you just run your fifteen miles a week. In fact, if you run *too* far, you may undermine the benefits of running. There's a limit to everything, even good things. For instance, some studies show that when the body is stressed close to its limit in long-distance running, there is a temporary suppression of the immune system. This makes the runner, for the moment, more prey to colds and viral infections. Of course, in the long run (please excuse the pun), your immune system will benefit from your exercise program because of the greater efficiency of your body. Then, too, when you stress your body too much, you are more prone to injuries—more on this in the next section.

The important thing to remember is that you are running only with and for yourself. You aren't competing with anyone else; you don't have to excel, and you run the distance that's right for you. If your friends can run farther and faster, that's great—for them. What's great for you is when you run your distance in your own way. Remember, in running everyone's a hero.

There are exceptions, however, and that is the runner who races. Races of ten kilometers, half-marathons, and marathons are very popular nowadays. Thousands of people take part in these races, which can be lots of fun. However, racing takes us beyond the scope of this book. If you want to find out more about it and the special training that may help you become a good racer, consult one of the many good books listed in the bibliography. This book is primarily for people who want to run with their dogs, and your dog almost certainly will not be wanted in a race!

Injuries—and How to Avoid Them

It's a common belief that runners incur lots of injuries, and there's some truth to it. Running makes the body work hard. Take the foot, for instance. Richard Schuster, M.D., was quoted in a *Los Angeles Times* article (August 23, 1981) as saying runners who weigh 150 pounds put 450 pounds of pressure on their feet with each step—more if they are heavier. Furthermore, each time we run a mile, we take eight hundred to one thousand steps. It's not surprising that runners come up with injuries; what is surprising is that they don't come up with many more! The fact that they don't is a tribute to the toughness and resilience of the body, and the amazing feet Mother Nature produced when she designed that humble but remarkable part of the body—the human foot. (That goes for a dog's foot too, by the way.)

It is fortunate that most of the injuries incurred by runners are minor and respond quickly to rest. Moreover, most of these injuries can be avoided by proper exercise and precautions. When runners observe these precautions, they rarely develop serious running injuries, and when they do hurt themselves, there usually was something wrong in the first place, or they didn't listen to their body and pushed it beyond its limit. What are these injuries and what can be done to avoid them?

Probably the four most common injuries are heel-spur syndrome, known technically as plantar iasciitis; runner's knee, alias chondro-malacia; shinsplints, which is an inflammation of the extensor muscles in the lower leg; and Achilles tendinitis, an inflammation of the powerful tendon that connects the lower posterior calf muscles to the foot.

Heel-spur syndrome is produced by repeated shock to the heel of the foot. It can usually be prevented by wearing proper footwear, because running shoes are designed to absorb shock. So if you're going to run, invest a little money in a pair of any of the excellent running shoes now available on the market. Invest in two pairs, in fact; it preserves the life of the shoes to alternate between the pairs. The surface on which you run is also important. Try to avoid running on concrete whenever possible. Asphalt is a little better, but dirt and grass are the best surfaces for running. They are resilient and will "give" slightly when your foot lands, thus mitigating some of the shock effect on your foot. True, you see lots of runners running on asphalt and even concrete, but remember, since you're going to run with your dog, you'll probably look for a place where your dog can run too—and that's not likely to be a city street.

Knee injuries are common, and sometimes serious, because the knee is such a vulnerable joint. Considering the difficult coupling of the thigh bone and the shin bone that are bound together in the knee, it is surprising there are not more difficulties. When Mother Nature devised the knee, she intended it primarily for walking and running, so it operates like a hinge. It is not, however, a simple hinge; it has some rotational and side-to-side angular movement to assist it in taking up the shock of running and walking. It is not designed for pronounced lateral movement, and this is what makes the knee so vulnerable in athletic competition.

Football and basketball players, for instance, often find their careers cut short because they were hit from the side and the knee didn't have enough sideways motion to absorb the shock. True, when you run, your knee mostly goes in a straight line, but sometimes there are subtle problems that get to the knee—and some of them begin with the foot.

The small joints of the foot, the ankle, the knee, the hip, and the lower back take up the force of running (or walking) and give us a smooth, even flow. When one of these determinants of gait is disturbed, the others must work overtime to take up the slack for the ailing one. Pronation of the feet is a common variant of running in which the arch of the foot is flat, which makes the foot roll inward. As a result, the foot often turns outward in relation to the leg axis and sometimes brings about a knock-knee tendency. Running causes the kneecap to slide off its track, which irritates and wears the slick, gliding, plastic, resilient cartilage on the kneecap's joint surface—producing what is called chondromalacia.

Sometimes the solution is as simple as getting the right pair of shoes. Many running shoes are designed to correct for pronation, but a shoe with the proper characteristic must be discovered. It helps to buy your footwear from an athletic shoe store with knowledgeable sales people who are interested in helping you find the right shoe for you. In certain cases you may need to go to your orthopedist or podiatrist who can prescribe an orthotic device for you that often will solve the problem.

Another cause of inflammation of the cartilage is too much shock. This comes when we run too far or when we run downhill. A runner going downhill places a great deal more shock on the knee than the runner who goes on level ground. If you develop pain in the knee, it is best to avoid the downhill terrain, or walk down a hill when you get to it.

Running on a consistently uneven surface can also mean trouble for the knee. For instance, people who run on city streets are running on a slight slant. When your foot hits the slanting surface, it automatically adjusts itself to keep your body straight, but this movement translates itself up to the knee, which doesn't have the flexibility of the foot, so it often becomes irritated when you log enough miles on this kind of surface. The solution? Run on flat surfaces. Oddly enough, rough surfaces seem to be okay. I run on rough dirt roads, even up rocky stream beds, with no problems. It's the constant running on a slant surface that seems to do the damage.

Knee problems also occur when the quadricep muscles (the big muscles of the thigh) are too weak. What makes the knee operate efficiently is the kneecap, or patella, and this is kept in its proper place by the quadricep muscles. When these muscles are too weak, the patella slides around as the knee is used, producing irritation of the cartilage. Exercises that strengthen the quadricep muscles usually prevent this from happening.

Shinsplints is a term loosely applied to any painful inflammation of muscles or tendons that usually occur in the lower part of the leg. They mainly come from too much stress and almost invariably respond quickly to rest and proper footgear.

Achilles tendinitis can be a more difficult malady to cure. For muscles to move bones they naturally have to be attached to the bones. Muscles, however, aren't attached directly to the bones but are attached by tendons. The Achilles tendon is perhaps the body's most important tendon because it attaches muscles to the heel: without it we couldn't walk. This tendon can become inflamed when it swells up, and becomes too tight for the sheath which encases it. This may produce incapacitating pain. Such inflammation occurs when the tendon is pulled too hard, too suddenly, or too often, because tendons have no stretch and therefore don't "give." What does give are muscles, which have a great capacity to stretch and contract. The way to avoid Achilles tendinitis, therefore, is to keep the muscles limber so they stretch sufficiently to absorb the force we place on them; otherwise this force will be applied to the unstretchable tendon.

A few simple exercises will help prevent Achilles tendinitis and other injuries. These exercises are valuable for anyone engaged in athletic activity, not just for runners, and even if you lead a sedentary life, you may want to do them just so your body won't atrophy completely. The five exercises that follow should do the job for the average runner, but if you need more, you can read the literature cited in the bibliography.

Exercise 1

Stand about two or three feet away from a vertical support (such as your car or a tree). Place your hands on the support and lean toward it with one foot about a foot and a half ahead of the other. Keeping your rear foot flat on the ground, bend that leg's knee. You should feel the pull this posture exerts on the powerful muscles that attach themselves to the Achilles tendon and this will keep those muscles limber and flexible.

Exercise 2

Still standing about three feet from the support, lean in with both feet together and flat on the ground. This will stretch your calf muscles.

Exercise 3

Keeping both legs straight, place one leg on top of something a few feet high—the bumper on your car will do. Lean in slightly. You will feel the big hamstring muscles on the posterior part of your thigh stretch as you do this. Lean in, gradually exerting more and more pressure until you feel a slight but not uncomfortable pain.

Exercise 4

Lie on your back, legs straight out. Raise your legs slightly and hold them a few inches off the ground. You will feel your stomach muscles tighten. This will strengthen them. Move your legs back and forth a few times in a "scissors" movement. Then raise your legs gradually over your head as far as you can comfortably. (Maybe you can touch the ground behind you and maybe you can't. Women are more limber at this than men.) This will strengthen and stretch the lower back muscles and the hamstrings. This may save you some day from having "lower back pain," a common ailment as we get older.

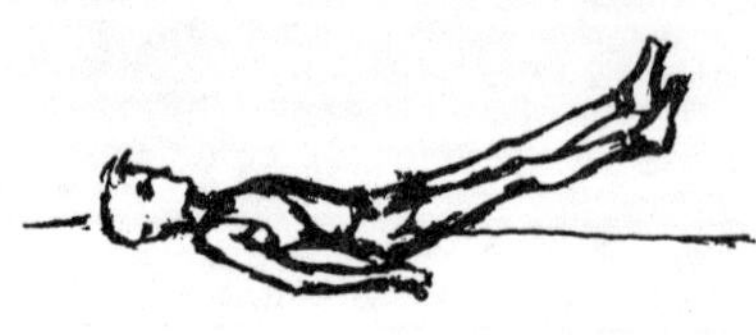

Exercise 5

Sit on a table, legs hanging down over the edge. Raise first one leg, then the other. After you've done this enough times you may want to add a small weight to your foot. This exercise will strengthen the quadriceps, those powerful thigh muscles that keep your kneecap in its proper place. You can also do this exercise by standing flat against a wall on one leg, raising the other leg as high as you comfortably can. You can also strengthen the quadriceps by climbing steep hills. If you don't have any steep hills nearby, try going up the stairs two at a time. If you work in an office building with an elevator, skip the elevator and go two at a time up the stairs instead. If your office is on the fiftieth floor, get out at the forty-fifth and walk up the last five flights.

Do these exercises two or three times each. Do them slowly and cautiously, and gradually stretch your muscles. A word of caution: Never "bounce." A bouncing movement might produce a minor muscle injury.

With the above precautions, you are not likely to injure yourself, but if you do there are certain steps you will need to follow. When you are injured, you will feel pain; that's the body's way of sending a message to the brain, and ultimately to you, that something is wrong. Pain is your body's way of talking, and your job is to listen to what your body is saying. There is an occasional minor pain that disappears after you run for a while, but if you are in pain and try running and the pain doesn't soon disappear, then stop. No more running until you are symptom free, unless your doctor says it's all right.

And that brings up the matter of your doctor. I've already suggested that you may want to consult your doctor before you begin running. If you have acute pain that doesn't disappear in a few days, you may want to consult a doctor who specializes in treating athletic injuries. This usually means a podiatrist or orthopedist. And remember once again that it's often important that the doctor to whom you go for running injuries is a runner. Otherwise your doctor may just declare that you have to stop running when it isn't really necessary. Once you have found a good doctor whom you trust, then follow the guidance of the two doctors in your life, your medical doctor and your own body, until they tell you it's safe to resume running.

Meanwhile, it's sometimes possible to engage in an alternate form of exercise, depending on the nature of the injury. Swimming is often prescribed for injured runners because the water supports the weight of the body. Bicycling is also often permissible because it doesn't have the jarring motion of running. Walking, too, may be possible.

RUNNING AND YOUR SAFETY

Running is a pretty safe way to spend your time. It's certainly a lot less dangerous than driving on the freeways, and it may even be safer than being at home, where it is said that more accidents take place than anywhere. However, there's no place where safety is absolutely guaranteed and there are precautions to take when you are running, just as there are for other activities in your life. Most accidents occur when you don't think there can be one. If you are conscious of the fact that you are in a situation where an accident could take place, you are on the alert and are able to prevent the possible mishap. So the best thing to do when running is to be aware of the potential hazards.

The biggest hazard, bar none, is the automobile. Of course, if you are running with your dog, you will probably have found a place to run where there are no cars—more on this later—so you will be a lot safer than the runner who jogs along a city street. Just the same, there will be times and occasions when you may have to run for a while along a road or cross an intersection. Here are some points to remember: Don't assume the drivers of approaching cars will see you; assume they won't and keep as far to the right as possible. Don't assume you are safe just because you are running on the shoulder of the road. The closest I ever came to being hurt running was when I was running well off to the side of the road in suburban Chicago at dusk and somebody in a big hurry decided to pass other cars using the shoulder. Of course he didn't see me, and I was lucky to get out of the way in time. Don't do what I did. Avoid running in or near traffic at dusk or dark when you possibly can. In fact, try not to run in the dark anywhere. You have to see where your foot is going to land—if it hits a rock or hole you may be in for a sprain or even a fracture. If you are crossing an intersection and a car is at the intersection waiting to cross or make a right or left turn, don't assume the driver sees you. Wave your hand at the driver, or even tap lightly on the hood of the waiting car to be sure you have the driver's attention. Even if the driver of the car does see you, don't assume he will respect your right to jog along the side of the road. Sadly, there are people who resent runners and like to harass them with their automobiles. I don't know why. Maybe they feel guilty or inferior because they are in such poor physical shape and you aren't. Whatever reason, there are characters who may sometimes give you a hard time. Finally, face traffic when you are jogging, just as you do when you are walking.

After all this you may decide against jogging on the street. If you do, you'll not only be safer but your dog will appreciate it too. He doesn't like to breathe in the fumes from automobile exhaust any more than you do.

I mentioned the nasty drivers who may decide to harass you when you are running. Unfortunately, there are certain characters in this world who constitute a special hazard to women. Usually runners make poor targets for a potential mugger. They just look too healthy to be easy victims. Besides, they seldom carry anything of value on them. But there are unfortunate incidents in which women have been sexually assaulted while they were running. A few safeguards might help prevent this from happening: If you drive to the place where you are going to begin your run, park your car in an open, public place where other cars and people are around. Don't take anything valuable with you, and don't leave anything valuable in your car. Whenever possible, run in places where there are other runners; it's the lone woman who is the target. Avoid running at dusk or dark unless you are sure you are in a safe place—that is, a place with other people around. If for any reason you are anxious (maybe it's getting dark or you see someone suspicious), don't hesitate to ask another runner if you can run with him or her. A woman runner will understand, and a male runner will feel flattered and protective. Finally, for added safety, run with your dog. If you have a good-sized dog with you, most attackers will avoid you and look for an easier mark.

RUNNING AND YOUR DIET

Enough of the gloomy side to the picture; back to the positive. I've already mentioned that running is excellent for weight control. It also is an education in how your body works. When you run, you learn about your body and come into a generally better relationship with it. As you do, you may find yourself altering your diet in a healthy direction. This is because running, like owning a dog, isn't just an isolated activity, it's part of a certain lifestyle that includes many things to help you be a healthier and more vital person.

If you eat a good diet, you'll find you feel better, run better, put on less unwanted weight, and enjoy your food more. The question is, what is a good diet? Not being a doctor or nutritionist, I'm no expert, which is a good thing for you, because most self-proclaimed experts seem to get pretty fanatical about food. However, I have read many recommended diets, including the one my own doctor recommends, and they all say one basic thing: Eat lots of fresh fruit and raw or lightly cooked vegetables, and cut down on animal fats. This means substituting fish or poultry for red meat much of the time, and keeping your use of dairy products down. A good diet also means eliminating or cutting down drastically on your consumption of processed sugar.

For hundreds of thousands of years, Mother Nature worked to perfect this body of ours, and for most of these years humankind ate a simple diet of nuts, grains, fruits, vegetables, fish, and lean meat. But in the last one hundred years people have been putting food into their bodies that wasn't intended for them to have, and processed sugar is one of these. The body makes glycogen out of most foods. Eat an apple and the body gradually breaks it down into sugar and stores the glycogen in muscle cells for energy. But processed sugar doesn't have to be gradually broken down; it hits the body all at once, and when a lot of sugar hits the bloodstream, the pancreas suddenly reacts with a violent release of insulin to correct what it perceives as an imbalance. The result is a loss of energy as the insulin depletes your body of the unwanted sugar, but it "overdoes" the job. In other words, there is a disturbance in your body's natural homeostasis, the ability to balance its inner chemistry, because it is overloaded with sugar.

Here's a rule of thumb for your diet: If it's a food God made, it's probably good for you; if it's a food man made, it probably isn't; and if it's a food that is advertised, it almost certainly isn't.

You may also want to add certain supplements to your diet. For instance, many people, including Nobel Prize winner Linus Pauling, think that ample Vitamin C strengthens your body's resistance to colds, other infections, and even cancer. Vitamin E may be especially important to you as a runner because it helps your blood cells carry their vital oxygen supply to all parts of your body. If you develop aching legs that keep you awake at night, it may be because your supply of Vitamin E is depleted and your blood cells can't properly replenish your muscle cells with oxygen. A calcium-magnesium supplement may also be helpful, especially if you find you are getting cramps after you run. Every time a muscle contracts and expands, it uses a bit of calcium, and magnesium is needed to enable the calcium to work. If you are having cramps, it may be that as a result of a depleted calcium supply, the muscles "fire" in a crazy, rather than rhythmic, way.

But if you eat a good diet, do you get enough vitamins and minerals anyway? Perhaps, and perhaps not. The problem is that when food is processed, cooked, or kept a long time after it is picked, it loses vitamins. Also, if fruits and vegetables are picked before they are ripe, which happens all the time so they won't spoil before they get to the consumer, they don't store up their proper nutrients, since this takes place in the last stages of ripening. If you want to get the maximum vitamin content from food, you have to pick the ripe fruit off the tree and eat it right away, and go down to your vegetable garden to pick, prepare, and eat your raw food salad immediately. Not many of us can do this, and this is one reason some people take vitamin supplements.

How much? Better ask your doctor or nutritionist or read a book written by an expert. Fortunately, with most vitamins it's hard to take too much since your body gets rid of what you don't need. Don't be deceived by the RDA (Recommended Daily Allowance) though. This is the amount of the vitamin you need to prevent overt disease symptoms such as scurvy or pellagra, not the amount that you, an active runner, need to function at optimum physical efficiency.

I haven't mentioned salt. That's because you don't need it, not even in hot weather. There's more than enough salt in our food and drinks to replenish the salt lost in perspiration.

Water's different. You use a lot of water when you run, especially when the weather is warm, and it is quite possible to get dehydrated. This seldom becomes a dangerous condition, but dehydration can leave you feeling depleted of energy. One way to tell if your body is low on water is to look at the color of your urine; if it's bright yellow you are probably dehydrated and need to drink more fluid. (The usual color of urine is about the color of straw.) The rule for running then, especially if it's warm and you are going to run a long distance, is to drink plenty of water before, during, and after your run.

Sometimes after a long run in hot weather, you drink and drink and still feel thirsty. This is called "after-thirst" and usually means that your body is short on electrolytes, those minute trace minerals essential to good body functioning. If you are eating fresh fruits and vegetables, just give your body a little time—it will soon replace the electrolytes you lost during vigorous exercise. If you get impatient, there are commercial electrolyte replacement drinks on the market that hurry the process of resupplying them.

So there it is. There's a lot more you could learn about the personal benefits of running, but this chapter should get you started. Put on your comfortable running shorts and get ready to go. Oh yes, don't forget your dog! Chances are he's right there with you, watching to see if you reach for your running shoes. As soon as you do, he begins to jump around. He's all excited and eager to go. That's one reason you'll enjoy him as a companion—he likes it so much. But there are some things you will need to know about running with your dog, just as there were some things you needed to know about running for yourself. So that's what we'll look at next.

3. The Why of Running with Your Dog

People suffer needlessly today because they have gotten too far away from their instincts and what is natural to them. As our intellects develop, we leave our bodies and souls far behind. To survive in this modern, tense world, we need to get in touch with what I call the "natural man" (or woman). If we do not connect with the natural person inside us, we remain split—one part is too far away from the other.

An analogy might help. The aircraft industry speaks of a "stretched out" version of a passenger airliner. They take a proven airplane and make it longer to accommodate more passengers. It still flies successfully because the cockpit, with its vital instrumentation, and the tail assembly, with its essential apparatus for giving the plane stability, are still soundly connected to each other. However, in many people today the conscious personality (the cockpit) and the more instinctive unconscious personality (the tail assembly) have grown so far apart that the connection between the two is often lost, or is tenuous at best. The result is a malaise of body and spirit.

Running, dancing, swimming, and certain other physical activities are helpful in restoring and maintaining the broken connection between mind and instinct. They are ways of healing the split that modern life forces on us. And for many of us, running with a dog is especially healing because it is such a natural thing to do.

We may not even be aware that we have lost contact with the instinctual person inside us. All we know is that we suffer from depressions, anxieties, meaninglessness, and addictions to life-defeating habits. But something in us—a part of us that was formed millions of years ago—knows that we are not living correctly. It's as though the very cells of our bodies remember.

My mother used to quote a poem to me. I don't know its source—she used to write poetry so she may have made it up herself. It goes like this:

A man has so much water in his hide,
He ought to surge with each incoming tide,
And all his cells like creatures of the deep,
Should glow with phosphorescence in his sleep.
And he should bellow like Leviathan
Though cast ashore on some wave's creamy span
And left to welter age and age ago
Great tidal forces in him still can flow
Sea water in his veins and tears of salt
His ears like conches roar within a vault
His heart revisits chasms drowned and dim
The Old Sea Mother still remembers him.

Scientists tell us a human's body fluids have the same chemical constituency as sea water. If our body cells could talk, they would tell us of our ancient origin in the primeval oceans. Something in us knows who we are and where we came from. It is important that we connect our conscious life to the deep, unconscious source of life within us. Then we are more complete, and our energy flows properly. For some people, one way to help do this is by running, and for some of them, running with a dog will add to this natural, healing activity.

I had an experience several years ago that impressed me with how natural it is to run with a dog. My great old running dog, Doc, had become too old to go with me on my once-a-week long run of thirteen to fourteen miles through the back country near San Diego, so I was making this run alone. One day I put my car in the parking lot at the lower end of San Clemente Park and began my stretching exercises in preparation for my long run up the canyon and into the wild country east of the park. When I was about to start, I saw two dogs coming helter-skelter down the hillside from the housing area above the canyon. One was a lusty young Setter, the other an equally energetic Pointer. I wondered as I began my run if their owners knew where they were. The dogs bounded ahead of me and disappeared into the woods; they evidently had escaped from their yard, I reflected, and were out to enjoy themselves in the canyon. After about a quarter of a mile of running, they reappeared from among the trees and crossed right in front of me. I admired their healthy, animal exuberance and continued on my way as they disappeared again. Not long afterward, they came back, racing within ten feet of me before bounding away into the tall grass on the other side of the path. So it went for mile after mile. I jogged slowly along, the dogs raced away, then returned close to me, then disappeared again. I finally realized that they were running with me!

Thirteen miles later I was back at my car, my two tireless companions trotting in just ahead of me. As I cooled down and got ready for the ride home, they sat there looking at me as though to say, "Aren't you going to run any more?" I admonished them sternly to go home, telling them their owners were probably frantic with worry and, although I had enjoyed running with them, they had gone far enough and should return home at once. As I drove off I saw them in my mirror, watching my car contemplatively as it disappeared.

Dogs are enthusiastic animals, and they need a time when they can express their natural exuberance. We can free ourselves from our staid, sober conventionality by sharing their exuberance with them. A run is a joyful time for a dog. As Barbara Woodhouse, the noted English dog trainer, pointed out in her book *No Bad Dogs*, dogs like excitement, and for a dog a run is full of excitement—new smells, new adventures, and the wonderful sensation of being free.

We also need excitement, and a dog's enthusiasm makes him a welcome running partner. J. Allen Boone, in his remarkable book *Kinship With All Life*, describes his long walks with Strongheart, the movie star dog he was caring for, on the isolated beaches of the Northwest. Boone writes:

> I never tired of being student-audience for him during these beach sessions. His zest for living . . . his vitality . . . his powerful and almost catlike agility . . . his enthusiasm . . . his sense of wonder and appreciation . . . his complete interest in the immediate thing he was doing . . . all these were delightfully educational and entertaining. He had a tremendous ability to extract fun, happiness and satisfaction out of each moment, and he never permitted life to become uninteresting, either for himself or for those around him.[1]

As we saw in the previous chapter, running is good for our health. There also is evidence that it is good for a dog's health. This is another reason to run with him: for his sake because he'll be healthier, and for our sake because it's more fun to have a healthy dog.

An article in the prestigious *New England Journal of Medicine*,[2] gives supporting evidence on the link between exercise and health in animals. The article discussed the relationship between an atherogenic diet and exercise in monkeys. An atherogenic diet is a diet that tends to clog the arteries with fatty material and produce conditions leading to heart disease and atherosclerosis. The experiment was designed to test any benefits of exercise on the health of monkeys.

The experiment was in two parts. First, twenty-seven monkeys were divided into three groups. Group One was given a carefully controlled diet with no exercise. Group Two was given an atherogenic diet with no

[1] J. Allen Boone, *Kinship With All Life* (New York: Harper & Row, 1954), p.58.
[2] Dieter M. Kramsch, Anita J. Aspen, Bruce M. Abromowitz, Toby Kreimendahl, and William B. Hood, Jr., "Reduction of Coronary Atherosclerosis by Moderate Conditioning Exercise in Monkeys on an Atherogenic Diet," *New England Journal of Medicine* (December 17, 1981).

exercise. Group Three was given an atherogenic diet with exercise. Observations were made over a period of three years and four months. At the end of this time, Journal Editor Robert A. Bruce cautiously concluded, the data "provided provocative and objective evidence that may support the protective value of periodic and regularly maintained moderate physical exercise."

In the second part of the experiment, certain of the young monkeys were given eighteen months of physical exercise prior to being put on an atherogenic diet for the ensuing twenty-four months. The prior exercise conditioning in the young monkeys was shown to have either delayed or prevented the coronary vascular disease induced by the atherogenic diet in the other monkeys. Specifically, the exercise increased the heart size, the left ventricular mass, and the diameter of the coronary arteries, and diminished the heart rate.

We don't want to exaggerate the health benefits exercise can give to our canine companions. It seems that dogs don't have the problem human beings and primates generally have with cholesterol clogging vital arteries. Many dogs, especially small ones, can probably get by with less exercise than people, at least as far as heart disease is concerned. Nevertheless, they do gain physical benefits from an appropriate exercise program.

Veterinarian Anna P. Clarke, in her column in the *Los Angeles Times*, received a letter asking what could be done to help an eleven-year-old dog suffering from heart disease. She answered:

> Heart disease occurs in about 10 percent of dogs, and 75 percent of those over 9 years of age. Unfortunately, it appears to be on the increase in dogs; obesity and lack of exercise are contributing to this rise.*

Her recommended treatment includes a planned exercise program commensurate with the remaining heart capacity of the particular dog.

*Anna P. Clarke, DVM, "Pet Doctor" *Home Magazine, Los Angeles Times* (January 24, 1982).

In addition to the physical benefits of running your dog, there are the psychological benefits. A dog that has an opportunity for exciting, exuberant exercise is likely to be steadier, happier, and less difficult than one that is confined and leads a sedentary life. When a dog doesn't have a chance to run, roam, experience new smells, and have his own canine experiences, he may become bored, lethargic, unstable, and even develop dangerous behavior.

Young dogs in particular need new locations and new experiences if they are to make a good life adjustment—just as people do. Dogs also need companionship with their masters, and running with your dog is an excellent way to strengthen this companionate relationship. The resulting bonding will also make your dog more responsive to your commands and generally more anxious to obey and please you.

One positive feature of running, as we have noted, is that it is an activity we can engage in alone. Unlike tennis, racquetball, or any similar sport, we don't need to find a partner, set a time, or reserve a court in order to run. Of course, sometimes we prefer to run with someone, but we don't have to, and many people welcome this, knowing that they can run whenever it pleases them and fits into their schedule. And if you do want a companion, your dog is always ready to go.

This is especially helpful to a woman because at times she may be afraid of running alone for fear of being attacked. But when a woman is running with a dog, she has a certain amount of protection, and can run with greater peace of mind. Most canines are naturally protective toward members of their own pack, and as far as your dog is concerned, you are a vital part of the pack. Almost any dog will react defensively when his or her master is threatened. Even if the dog simply barks loudly, such protective behavior will deter many a would-be assailant. Why attack a person accompanied by a dog that may cause problems when an easier victim may be around the corner?

Some dogs make better protective companions than others. A large dog—sixty-five pounds or more—offers more protection than a small one. Certain breeds, such as Airedale Terriers, German Shepherds, Dobermans, Great Danes, Rhodesian Ridgebacks, Rottweilers, Labrador Retrievers, and Shorthaired Pointers, are more impressive guard dogs than Poodles or Cocker Spaniels. It isn't necessary to have a vicious dog to benefit from having a dog as a protective running companion. It's enough when a dog looks the part.

For a year Doc and I ran regularly with a Doberman Pinscher. The dog belonged to one of my daughter's friends, who left him with us temporarily. I was glad to have him run with us, for he and Doc made good running companions. The Doberman was a strong, large animal, who was so fierce looking that I used to reassure people as I ran past that he was friendly. The truth was, the Doberman had the heart and soul of a pussy cat. He wouldn't have hurt a fly, but to look at him you never would have guessed it. If I had been a woman running alone, my Doberman Pinscher companion would have reassured me greatly.

A good guard dog can be either male or female; they are equally protective and courageous. They do, however, need to be mature. A young dog is too innocent to be protective against dangers. Your dog's guarding instinct will not emerge until he reaches puberty, and probably will not be developed until he is one or two years old. If your young dog is super friendly and you despair that he will never be a guard dog, don't lose hope. This trait often develops almost overnight when the time is right.

It should be reiterated that you do not need or want a vicious dog. If your dog, out of aggressiveness or even sheer exuberance, barks at or charges other people when you are running, he must be curbed. If your dog is especially protective, these basically desirable qualities may have to be properly shaped by you, the owner, to protect other people and, for that matter, protect you from a lawsuit. Occasionally, as joggers know, dogs like to race out and snap at the flying legs of runners. This quality must certainly be stopped when it develops. However, my experience is that dogs who run with their owners get used to people jogging and don't display this characteristic. It is the bored dogs who hang around home and are startled to see a jogger going by that are likely to be the problem.

My daughter likes to run with her dog, and one reason is for protection. The best place to run in her neighborhood in Orange County, California, is on a trail along the Santa Ana River, but in places this trail is isolated and it gets pretty lonely out there. So she takes her dog along. To reach the river trail she has to go through a developed area, and here she has her dog on a leash, but once she reaches the river she lets it run free. She and her dog think this is a good idea, quite reasonable and proper, but the local animal control officer sometimes has other ideas, and once he intercepted her just as she was taking her dog off the leash and gave her

a stern warning. One day as she was about to start her river run with her Great Dane/German Shepherd free again, she saw the officer approaching in his truck. She had the leash on her dog again in no time. When the officer came up to her, he greeted her approvingly and the two chatted together in a friendly way before she resumed her run. As she jogged away, dog beside her, the officer called after her, "And when you run along here, don't forget: always take your dog with you."

The bottom line of running with your dog, however, is that it must be pleasurable. As we noted, when we do something we are created to do, it's enjoyable. It is the same for our dog as it is for us. Dogs were made to run—and most of us are too. For J. Allen Boone, the joy he felt when roaming with Strongheart was a mystical experience:

Neither of us was expressing himself as an original thinker
or an independent source. On the contrary, we were being
communicated through by the Mind of the Universe. We
were being used as living instruments for its good
pleasure. That primal, illimitable and eternal Mind was
moving through me to Strongheart, and through
Strongheart to me. Thus I came to know that it moves
through everything everywhere in a ceaseless rhythm of
harmonious kinship.*

When I start a run with my Labrador Retriever, and she jumps into the
air out of sheer exuberance, I think I know a little bit of what Boone was
describing.

*Boone, *Kinship With All Life,* p.76.

4.   When to Start (And When to Stop, Too)

In trying to determine how old a dog should be before it is safe to start him on his running career, I read everything I could find on the subject, and talked to a lot of veterinarians. I found the answers varied widely. Some told me a dog can be only a few months old, others said the dog should be two years old.

It shouldn't be surprising that authorities can't agree on this point because it's the same as trying to determine the age people should begin running. Some people think nothing of having their eight-year-old child run in the ten-kilometer race—or even a marathon. Others throw up their hands in horror at such an idea, and argue that a child's bones are too green at that age to be subjected to such stress. And the doctors disagree just as much as everyone else.

I suppose this means we must decide for ourselves when we will start running our dog. The following are some facts that can help guide us in making a decision about when our dog is ready to start running.

It takes about six months for a dog's skeletal growth to reach its maximum development, and about a year before the dog has reached its complete growth. A rule of thumb in reckoning a dog's age is to calculate the first year of a dog's life as equivalent to seventeen human years, and each year after that as equal to five more. This is only a rough approximation, since a large dog, on the average, will not live as long as a small dog. (The life expectancy of Great Danes, for instance, is about eight years, but a Cocker Spaniel may live to be sixteen.) Still, this gives us a rough guideline, and since a child isn't physically mature until the late teens, we can see why some people recommend waiting a full year before subjecting a dog to the stress of long-distance running. Even then, however, the dog's bones may not be fully hardened, which may be the reason some people say to wait until a dog is two years old before running him very far.

We mustn't expect too much of our puppy and try to train him too early. Just as we would not want or expect our three-year-old child to run five miles with us, so we shouldn't expect our three-month-old pup to be ready to run. Puppies need to romp and play and to do plenty of running around as they do so, but on their own time and in their own way. The sustained running can wait until later, until the pup is a young dog and has attained a certain amount of physical and psychological maturity.

One fairly safe way to proceed is to wait until the dog is six months old, then begin to take him on short runs, getting him used to the idea and developing his physical conditioning. As the dog matures, the length of his run can gradually be extended. By the time he is fully developed he will be in shape to go on the long runs with you.

This, of course, is a general rule. We need to take into account the different breeds of dogs and the characteristics of individual animals. Some dogs are bred for running, and some animals will run more readily than others. As with people, readiness for running will vary according to individual circumstances.

Greyhounds, Salukis, and Whippets are bred specifically for running; they are coursers, and are naturally endowed with the ability to run easily and swiftly in open pursuit of quarry. There should be no difficulty in running these dogs, except that they may not stay close to you. It is their

instinct to race after their quarry, and their master's job is to keep up with them.

Other strong runners are the hunting breeds, including Pointers and Setters of all types, Vizslas, Weimaraners, and any kind of hound. The water dogs, such as Retrievers and Spaniels, are less strong runners. Airedale Terriers are also strong runners. All these dogs are generally well put together and capable of taking a lot of punishment without injury.

Working dogs, such as German Shepherds, Great Danes, Doberman Pinschers, Collies, and Boxers, are also strong animals and can take a lot of exercise, providing they are free of injuries and disease. This can be a problem, for instance, with German Shepherds, which often have congenital hip dysplasia problems, which will be discussed later.

Other working dogs are also strong, but may not be the greatest runners over a long distance. These include Huskies, Samoyeds, Saint Bernards, and Newfoundlands, which are enormously strong, but not swift. The same is true of people. For instance, no one would expect a 285-pound guard on the professional football team to make a good marathon runner, although he's hard to stop when he charges you at full speed while clearing the path for a ball carrier.

Although short-legged dogs are probably more enthusiastic runners, they are more limited in their capacity to run. That's understandable. If our legs were as short as a Dachshund's, we would get pretty tired too, after we had run a few miles. If you have a short-legged dog, take him with you on your run by all means, but watch him carefully. If he gets exhausted when you run him six miles, take him with you on your three-mile jaunts.

Which dog is best for you as a running companion will depend on what kind of running you do. Remember that dogs vary individually, as well as in terms of their breed. Sexually, however, there is little difference. Females and males are equally strong runners. Females have the added advantage of sticking to you more closely than males, and they seldom fight with other dogs. More about this later.

In my many years of running, I've run with many different types of dogs. I've already mentioned my Retriever/German Shorthaired Pointer mix, Doc. In his prime Doc was an enthusiastic and tireless runner. I can never recall Doc's becoming exhausted before I did. On my

longest runs—up to twenty miles—Doc was spirited all the way. And, of course, if I ran twenty miles, he ran thirty because his course was to zig-zag over the terrain in pursuit of rabbits and other excitement.

For about three years, I had an Airedale bitch that ran with Doc and me. She, too, was a strong and tireless runner. The two of them used to be halfway across the county before I could get out of the car. She was a great dog, but developed a trait I couldn't live with: antagonistic behavior toward the two-year-old boy who lived nearby. Sadly, I could not let this beautiful animal live and she had to be put to sleep.

I have already mentioned the Doberman that ran with me for a year. He also was a fine, strong animal, but not quite up to the long-distance running that Doc could handle. Anything up to fifteen miles was fine with him.

For several years my daughter had a Great Dane/German Shepherd. She was a strong, exuberant animal. I often ran with her and my daughter and never knew the dog to tire, although I don't recall ever running twenty miles with her.

I now have a Yellow Labrador Retriever. At seventy pounds, Cori's the biggest Lab I have ever seen, and heavy muscled. She's not quite as durable a runner as Doc was, but she's a good runner—and just as enthusiastic. I began running short (quarter-mile) distances with her when she was a few months old, mainly to train her to stay with me. Not that she needed much training, for it's her instinct to stick close by. When she was six months old, she was ready for longer jaunts, such as four miles. Now she runs with me as far as I want to go.

Those of you who remember the cautious advice I gave a few pages earlier about training pups will perceive that I didn't follow my own advice with Cori. That's correct, but I did introduce her to running cautiously and watched carefully for any sign of injury or undue fatigue. It was only after I was satisfied that this particular dog could handle it that I started on the longer runs.

How far to run your dog is not just a matter of age, however; it's also a matter of conditioning. No matter how old a dog is, he shouldn't be running long distances with you until he is in the proper shape for it. When you started running, you didn't start out with ten miles. You ran one mile at first, perhaps—maybe even less—and only gradually increased your distance. When you felt an injury, you stopped until it healed itself. When you felt flat, you let a day or two go by before you ran again. Maybe it took a year to build up to the point where you felt okay about running five or ten miles. It's the same way with your dog. If you have a dog, young or old, who is not used to running, you will want to start out with short runs and gradually build up. You will want to observe the dog carefully. When there is any sign of limping, a paw injury, or undue fatigue, you will want to lay off. When the symptoms persist, have a vet examine him. But don't be too cautious. Remember, your dog is probably a strong animal. Chances are that pretty soon he'll be able to outrun you. Dogs don't need to be coddled when they are in shape. They enjoy the robust exercise, and like to get worn out doing it.

It's hard to know when to start a dog running, and it's also hard to know when to stop. Sooner or later old age catches up with all of us— dogs and people alike—and there comes a time when we have to slow down and not run so far. I have mentioned Doc's tireless running, but as the years went by it became apparent that he was no longer up to the long runs he handled with such ease in his youth. By the time he was nine years old, it was evident that he couldn't keep up with me on my longest runs, and much to his dismay I had to leave him behind, but I still took him for runs up to eight miles. Then, as he reached ten and eleven years of age, the distances he could run without discomfort became less and less. I took him on runs of up to four miles, however, right up to a few months before his death at the age of thirteen. It was hard to leave him behind. He would watch me like a hawk, and if he saw me putting on my running gear, he would start to wag his tail eagerly. Even when he was quite an old man, he would stagger to his feet gamely, ready to run in spirit even though his somewhat arthritic old body could no longer keep up, and he would look at me reproachfully when I left without him.

I mentioned Doc's arthritis. It wasn't bad, but you could tell he had some because he walked rather stiffly when he was old, and he whimpered some in the evening when he had too much exercise. On the other hand, moderate exercise helped him. Arthritis is one of the problems you have to look for in your aging dog, and in a later chapter I will have more to say about this and other ills your dog can incur. For now, however, let's take a look at some of the special training your dog may need if he is to be a safe and enjoyable running partner.

5. Training Your Dog to Run with You

If you want to dislike your dog, and have other people dislike him too, neglect his training. A well-trained dog is a pleasure, and a good companion at home or on the running path. Training is always important, but if you run with your dog it's more important than ever.

You will want to begin with ordinary obedience training. While still a young animal, your dog should learn the essential things: to come when called, to sit, to stop on command, not to jump up on people, and to walk at heel. There are a number of good books on obedience training, so there is no need for me to duplicate their good advice.

A book, however, can only generalize training techniques. You may also wish to enroll yourself and your dog in an obedience class. The professional dog trainer who runs the class can help you find the best way to train your particular dog. For instance, if you have a dominant type dog—one who tends to carry his tail up—he will present certain problems. He'll need to learn that *you* are the "alpha dog," the dominant one in his "pack." Otherwise he'll dominate you. On the other hand, if your dog is excessively submissive—the tail-tends-to-go-down variety— then you will need to use especially gentle albeit firm techniques or the dog will be too cowed to learn. Another value of obedience classes is the opportunity for your dog to become socialized to other dogs and people, which will be a special asset when you run with him. If either you or your dog is a really difficult character, it's also possible to engage the services of a private dog trainer, who will come to your house and give you the individual attention you may need.

I referred to the fact that you might be a difficult owner because training a dog is largely a matter of training the owner. You, the owner, need to have clearly in mind the kind of behavior you want from your dog. You also need to have clearly in mind how to patiently but firmly get your dog to do what you want. You will need to understand the mind of the dog. A dog learns by association, tending to repeat patterns of behavior that he associates with something pleasurable, and avoid patterns of behavior that bring something unpleasant with them. He connects things in his mind—"this behavior brought something I liked; this behavior did not." If you remember this, and have the right mental attitude, training your dog is not going to be difficult, for dogs are intelligent animals. They learn remarkably fast and are eager to please you. Furthermore, they want you to be in charge of the situation, and feel more secure when they know that you are the master, even though at times, like children, they may display what we would regard as willful behavior.

However, there are a few special problems you will encounter if you run with your dog, and since even the best books on dog training don't discuss special running problems, I will make a few comments about the particular situations you as a person who runs with your dog might face.

Your dog may develop the unpleasant habit of getting in front of you in such a way that you have to break your stride to avoid running into him. I have talked to at least one dog owner who reported that he had to give up running with his dog for this reason. When this happens, bump or even kick your dog as he starts to get in front of you, and as you do so, give a sharp verbal command for him to move out of the way. The combination of the physical reprimand with your verbal correction will make it possible later to use only the verbal signal. Remember to keep the verbal

command short and simple—no long sentences or expletives, just a vigorously stated "away!" or similar command. Remember, also, that if your dog is a herding type dog, such behavior comes naturally to him, and a special amount of training may be necessary to counter his instinct. It may also help to begin by running the dog with a leash. In this way he will learn the proper position to take relative to you. Don't be afraid that you may hurt your dog if you bump or kick him. Dogs are tough and it will take more than one or two kicks to do any damage. But your dog won't like it, and should soon learn to avoid that dangerous area in front of you. Remember that dogs learn by association. Running in front of you and getting close to your legs means an unpleasant kick in the ribs and the verbal indication of your displeasure.

As I mentioned, you won't hurt your dog, but you will need to be careful not to hurt yourself. When you break your stride to bump into or kick your dog, you could lose your balance if you're not careful. Keep this in mind and start out guardedly when you discipline your dog to keep him from running too close to you.

If it sounds cruel to talk about kicking your dog, remember that it's much less cruel than rejecting your dog because you aren't able to be firm with him. Your dog doesn't want you to dislike him, and he doesn't want to cause you a problem, but you will dislike him if he keeps running in front of you. Proper, firm training to discourage this bad habit (or any other bad habit for that matter) is a kindness to the animal, not cruelty. But you must be consistent. Don't let your dog run in front of you one day but not the next, for this only confuses him.

A more difficult version of this same problem occurs when the dog runs too closely *behind* your legs, for it's possible for your legs to become entangled with the dog, unexpectedly tripping you. It's also harder to see the dog behind you and therefore easier to be unaware of the danger. When this happens, the same principle applies. Make it unpleasant for the dog to run too close to your legs by letting your legs fly back at him when he runs behind you. But the same warning applies here. Start out gradually so you learn how to do it without losing your balance and taking a bad fall.

Your running dog will need to know all the usual dog commands, but an especially important one is "Stop!" This may not be a necessary command for people who keep their dogs in the backyard, but out in the open it may save your dog's life if he has been trained to respond instantly to your "Stop!" command, even though he may be some distance from you.

Any good obedience training book will tell you how to train your dog to stop on verbal command, but in the field the command should be given by both the voice and a proper hand signal. There may be times when you are running when your voice command may be inaudible to your dog because he's too far away, or there is too much competitive sound from traffic or other disturbances.

Suppose, for instance, that you are on one side of a road and your dog is on the other side. The dog is coming back to you, but you can see approaching traffic. "Stop!" may now be an essential command for your dog to have learned. Because of the noise of the approaching traffic, it may be important for your dog to have learned to obey your hand signal to stop as well as your verbal command. Instant obedience will be required even though the dog is coming back to you, which is probably what he thinks he should be doing at that moment.

If your dog is on a leash, this command is not necessary, and the above situation could not arise. This brings up the question of whether to run your dog on a leash or let the dog run free.

There are a lot of advantages to running with your dog on a leash. It will be generally safer. It will certainly guarantee that your dog stays with you and will prevent the two of you from becoming separated. It will also ensure that your dog is running legally, except in places where even leashed dogs are forbidden, such as most beaches in the summer.

If you decide to run with your dog on a leash, you will want to teach the dog to heel. Instructions on training a dog to walk at heel are readily available, and it is not difficult to teach most dogs to walk alongside of you when on a leash without lagging behind or pulling ahead. After you have taught your dog to walk at heel, it's a simple procedure to expand the training to running. In fact, once trained to walk at heel the dog will probably automatically run at heel as well.

Running with your dog on a leash has so many advantages that many people may wish to run this way all the time. But there is one marked disadvantage. The leash inhibits the freedom of movement of both dog and runner. Dogs like to run free, and this is particularly true of a hunting

type dog whose instinct is to roam and nose about here and there in search of enticing little animals to chase. The trappings of civilization that require such a dog to be leashed may often be necessary, but they are always a cramping restriction. It's asking a lot to make a robust dog always have his freedom of movement restricted. And if you are like I am, you want to be free too when you run, and not cramped by having to hold on to a leash with a dog at the other end of it. If you feel this way, you may wish to run most of the time, or at least some of the time, with your dog running free.

If this is your decision, you will face the problem of finding special places in which to run. You will want to find a location where it is safe and legal for your dog to run unleashed, or—if not legal technically, at least a place where nobody cares. And you will certainly want to be extra careful that your dog is properly licensed, and wears a collar with an identification tag on it with the dog's name and your phone number.

In San Diego there are two places within the city limits where dogs are allowed to run without a leash. One is a portion of Ocean Beach called "dog beach," for obvious reasons. The other is an undeveloped island in Mission Bay, four miles around and reached only by a single causeway, known as Fiesta Island. Fiesta Island is one of the ugliest places I've seen.

Low, flat, undeveloped, it is covered with sand or unappealing, bushy vegetation, and inhabited only by jack rabbits (which dogs love to chase, by the way). But the dogs don't know it's ugly, and precisely because it is such a scroungy place it's also a place where you and your dog can do about whatever you want and nobody is going to complain. For this reason it's also a kind of beautiful place. My daily prayer is that the City Fathers will never decide to "fix it up."

Because it's okay to have your dog unleashed on Fiesta Island, and it's a fairly safe place too, with traffic restricted to the single road around it, that's where my dog and I often run. But I like variety when I run. It's more interesting when you run one day in one place and another day somewhere else. So I've found other places to run as well.

One of these other places, which I mentioned earlier, is San Clemente Canyon Park on the outskirts of the city. Technically, you're supposed to have your dog leashed in San Clemente Park, but nobody seems to care. I was once stopped there by an animal control officer and was certain I would be fined, or at least scolded because Doc was running free, but he only wanted to be sure my dog was properly licensed. (He was.) It's a good, safe place to run with a dog. Moreover, beyond the boundaries of the official park are many country roads and trails that are off-limits to automobiles, but perfect for running if you don't mind a few rocks on the path now and then. You can run for miles back there and never meet another human being. This is the place I was running when the two dogs joined me for the sake of the run and hunt together.

The back country beyond San Clemente Canyon Park is a perfect place to run except for one thing: rattlesnakes in the spring and summer. But more about this later.

It has taken me a while to find the places in or near my city where I can run with my dog off a leash, but I've managed to find them. Chances are that you can find such places in your city too if you look hard enough.

If you let your dog run free, special problems may develop. One is the ever-present possibility that you and your dog may become separated. This possibility is stronger with certain breeds than others, and stronger if you have a male rather than a female. Hunting dogs—like my dog Doc—are especially likely to take off into the fields, woods, and bushes. Working dogs, like Shepherds, are more likely to stay right by you.

You will need to observe your dog's characteristics. Doc, a great hunter and roamer on our runs, who often pursued a rabbit for a half-mile with great enthusiasm, also always found his way back to me and seemed to have a kind of radar that enabled him to know where I was. I learned with time that I could trust Doc to be as concerned with finding me after a roaming jaunt through the country as I was to find him. Certain breeds, however, may give you more trouble, and one of them is a Beagle. This redoubtable little hound has a reputation for becoming so enthusiastic about his hunting that he forgets all about you. If this is the case, you may have a problem, for it's no fun to finish your run and be unable to locate your dog.

It is the unneutered dog that has the strongest instinct to roam. There's no doubt that testosterone will influence your dog's behavior and may create problems, so if you really have difficulty, you may want to consider having your dog neutered. You may also want your female spayed, for obvious reasons, and in my experience spaying your female doesn't alter her personality. It is sometimes said that a spayed female tends to put on more weight, but running her and proper diet should take care of that problem. However, neutering the male will change your dog's personality; not necessarily for the worse, but it will be different. Personally, I like my male dogs the way God made them and prefer to take my chances with testosterone.

If you're going to let your dog run free, you'll want to have "come" commands that the dog can hear at a distance. Since the human voice doesn't carry all that far, this means you will have to find "come" signals besides your voice call. The simplest is a quick clap of the hands. When you clap your hands sharply together you make a sudden, decisive sound that will carry farther than your voice and will instantly attract your dog's attention if he is within earshot. He soon learns to look up at you when you clap your hands, and if you then encourage him to come, clapping your hands repeatedly as he does so, you will find you have taught him an effective "come" command that will be useful for your running.

But sometimes your dog is too far away to hear even your hand clap. Whistling—or even better, using a whistle—is then a great help. I've used both methods, but the regular whistle has the advantage of being heard at a considerable distance. With Doc, I could bring him back from a half-mile away by giving my two-whistle-blasts-together call. It was always a thrill to see him bounding up out of the woods or brush in response to this signal. It's easy to teach. First teach him to come by ordinary methods, then, as he comes toward you give him your whistle call. He soon learns to associate the whistle sound with coming to you.

Remember, however, always to use the same type of whistle blast— two sharp ones close together works well—and also always to use the same whistle. Buy an ordinary five-and-dime store whistle so if you lose it you can replace it with another just like it. You could also use one of those dog whistles that the dog can hear but you can't, but I like the reassurance when I blow on my whistle of knowing it is making a sound. You can also buy training whistles at most pet shops. They are extra loud and are used in field training, and some models come in pretty colors to boot.

When you run with an unleashed dog who likes to roam from time to time, get in the habit of always running your route the same way. Don't run your favorite route counter-clockwise one day and the other way another day. Dogs soon learn the route you are running. They will know it by heart, just as you do, and therefore will know where to find you should you become separated. Always leave your car parked in the same place too. If you reach the end of your run and are waiting by your car you will have the satisfaction of knowing that your dog knows where to come and look for you.

If all this talk about getting separated from your free-running dog makes you anxious, remember that it seldom happens. Even with free-roaming Doc we were seldom apart for more than a few minutes. It is the instinct with most dogs to stay close by their masters, and with most dogs that instinct is so strong you never need to worry. The dog I run with now, Cori, my Yellow Labrador Retriever bitch, is right by my side almost all of the time, no matter where we are. Even if she goes off after a rabbit, she never goes so far that she loses sight of me. So it's not a big problem, but if a problem does develop, you need to know how to deal with it.

Why put up with these possible problems at all? Maybe you shouldn't. Maybe a leash is your way. As for me, I guess I just need to watch something in life be absolutely free now and then, and my dogs have been elected. They seem as happy about the arrangement as I am. Just the same, it does increase the hazards. We've dealt with one hazard in this chapter—getting separated—and in the next chapter we'll deal with some more.

6.　　　　Hazards—And What to Do About Them

Besides the danger of getting separated, other hazards of running with your dog include cars, snakes, wild animals, ticks, foxtails, other dogs, and cuts. These are hazards for any dog, but when you run with a dog, special circumstances can develop.

Cars

Cars are by far the worst hazard. The problem is that dogs have no instinct to protect themselves from the automobile. A dog that will shy away from a bird rustling in a bush, will dash heedlessly in front of a three thousand pound car. The only perfectly safe way to run with your dog is to avoid running where there are cars. Since we have seen that cars are also the greatest hazard for you, it seems like a good idea all the way around to avoid running any place where there is fast-moving traffic.

Remember that dogs can react unexpectedly. The fact that a dog has never run out into the road when a car is coming doesn't mean that he never will. Something unexpected may come up—a rabbit across the road, a bitch in heat—and your dog who never before went into traffic may dash across six lanes of a busy highway.

Dogs have no instinct to protect them, but they can learn. Doc, when he was about a year old, dashed up the side of the apparently safe canyon we live next to, and across the busy street. A truck weighing about five thousand pounds drove completely over him. He emerged unhurt on the other side. To be sure, he could hardly walk for three days because he was so stiff and sore, but there were no broken bones and no internal injuries. Of course he was lucky—he passed between the wheels. After that I had no trouble with Doc and moving vehicles. At the sound of one approaching he shied away. But Doc was a smart dog, and some dogs don't seem to learn even when they've been hit.

It is best to try to anticipate danger from cars. I've already mentioned Fiesta Island in San Diego, a place where you can let your dog run free. It's a pretty safe place, but there *is* a road around it, and a dog could get hit. I always tried to park on the inland side of the road, so when my dog was set free from the car he would start sniffing around toward the center of the island and away from the traffic. However, the San Diego police forbade parking on that side of the road and now I have to park on the other side. This means the dog has to cross the road to get to where it is interesting while I am doing my stretching exercises. As I said, if there are cars around, there is no absolutely safe place for you or your dog. The best you can do is try to anticipate trouble.

SNAKES

So it's always going to be safe if you go where there aren't any cars. Right? Wrong. Because, at least in Southern California, if you go where there are no cars you are going to find rattlesnakes. I have already described the fine back-country places to run that I have discovered in the San Diego area. Within ten or fifteen minutes of downtown these canyons and mesas, with their miles of dirt roads, make a great place for a man or woman and dog to have a long romp. There's a lot of wildlife too. I've seen deer, coyotes, rabbits, hawks, skunks, and oppossums. Unfortunately there are also rattlesnakes.

Make no mistake about it: if you live in the Southwest where there is the kind of food snakes like, such as rabbits and mice, there are likely to be rattlesnakes. In the winter, snakes are no problem, for they are cold-blooded creatures and in the winter they hibernate or become so sluggish they're no threat. But from late March through the summer they are moving about, and I've come across a number of them.

I'm not concerned for myself; I see the snakes as they are crossing the road. It's not hard to spot them before I run into them, and rattlesnakes are not interested in attacking or running a person down; they bite only in defense. The dog, however, will not notice the snake unless it's moving. If the snake is moving, the dog may come up to it out of curiosity to investigate. Or a dog that runs through the brush on the side of the road could stir up a rattlesnake. Snakes have no scent. This helps because the dog will not smell the snake and decide to sniff it out. On the other hand, it also means the dog could run right into a motionless snake and never know it was there. As with cars, the dog has no instinct that will protect it against a snake, and if the dog should get bitten, it may not live to learn from its experience.

Fortunately, dogs have more physical resistance to rattlesnake venom than people do. Dogs can get bitten and still survive, even though they are usually not as big as people (the larger the victim, the more likely he is to survive a rattlesnake bite).

If your dog should get bitten, there are things you can do to help. If the bite is on a leg, a tourniquet will slow the progress of the venom through the dog's body. Remember, the idea is not to shut off the flow of blood, which would be extremely dangerous for the dog, but only to shut off the lymphatic drainage. Therefore, the tourniquet should not be too tight. You should be able to insert your finger between the tourniquet and the dog's hide. Of course, if the bite is on the nose or face a tourniquet is out of the question.

The next thing you will want to do is get the dog to an animal hospital that has anti-venom. Carry the dog, or go get help; you don't want him to run. That would mean almost certain death if he had any distance to go. If you run where there are snakes it also helps to find out in advance what animal hospitals store the anti-venom, because not every veterinarian will have it immediately available in his office. Also you need to know in advance where the twenty-four-hour emergency facilities are, since your dog might be bitten before or after normal veterinarian working hours.

Be sure not to be too over-zealous in your first aid. Cutting over the fang marks is not recommended. It will do little good, and you could permanently lame your dog by cutting some vital nerves. The anti-venom and your dog's natural capacity to overcome the effects of the poison are your best aids.

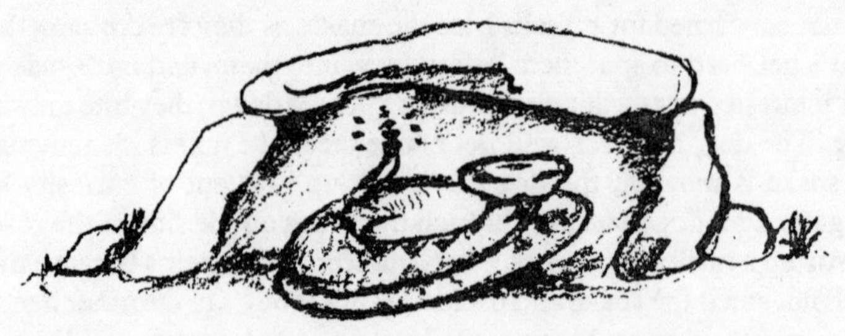

Your dog can get bitten hiking as well as running. One day my brother, my daughter, and I, along with my dog Doc, and her Great Dane/German Shepherd Gracie, hiked on Santa Rosa Mountain in Southern California at an elevation of eight thousand feet. According to the books, there aren't supposed to be any rattlesnakes at this elevation, but one Mojave Diamondback hadn't read the script. The two dogs, my daughter, and I passed within two feet of a deadly Mojave rattlesnake and didn't know it. However, when my brother went by, it was more than the snake could handle and it set up a terrific rattling. It was so well hidden underneath a rock it took us quite a while to spot it in spite of the noise it was making. I don't know exactly how big it was—nobody wanted to reach a hand under the rock to pull it out—but judging from the thickness of the body, which appeared to be about as thick as my wrist, it was big enough to have done a lot of damage.

Do I have you scared now? Maybe you should be. I must confess, for the sake of my dog, I avoid snake country once spring arrives. Just the same it's surprising how seldom people and dogs get bitten by rattlesnakes. Not too long ago I was walking with Cori along a well-traveled path in San Clemente Canyon where I'd never seen a snake before. Cori was running ahead of me about twenty feet when suddenly I heard the unmistakable noise of a rattlesnake—I say unmistakable because once you've heard that sound you never mistake it for anything else—and there was Cori on the path, nose pointed toward the grass at the edge, where that wonderful, terrible sound was coming from. Of course I hurried to the scene and grabbed Cori by the collar. I peered into the grass and there was a magnificent Western Diamondback—a really

good specimen—all coiled up and rattling away. Cori's attitude seemed to be, "I don't know what this funny creature is that's making all the racket but I think I'll just keep my distance." The rattlesnake's attitude seemed to be, "I'm not looking for trouble but if you insist on jumping at me I'll have to bite." My attitude toward the snake was, "Everybody has a right to be out here, including you, so I'm just going to go on my way and leave you alone." And off we went. Sure, snakes can be a problem in certain parts of the country, but I still feel safer with my dog on Santa Rosa Mountain or in San Clemente Canyon than I do on a freeway in my car.

WILD ANIMALS

Skunks are more of an annoyance than anything else and are not likely to be encountered on the trail. They are nocturnal and once the sun is up they are supposed to be home in bed. But if you run at dawn or dusk you could fine one, and you don't have to be out in the country, either, for skunks have found a way to get along just fine right in your favorite suburb. If your dog gets sprayed it's a problem, but a bath in tomato juice—that's right, tomato juice—does wonders. And your dog usually *will* learn. Doc was sprayed twice, and then he decided that not every black and white little animal was a cat that had to be chased.

Other wild animals seldom constitute a threat. Coyotes, for instance, have been known to come into settled areas at night, entice a dog away, and kill it. They kill cats that way as well, and since the coyote is a resourceful animal who has learned how to live in proximity to people, he can be dangerous to your pet Poodle. Coyotes are not a threat when you are running, partly because they are mostly nocturnal and seldom around during daylight hours, and partly because they will shy away from a human being. I have seen them many times on my runs around San Diego and there has never been any difficulty, although my dog's hair certainly rises on his back when he runs across a fresh coyote scent.

Life has all kinds of dangers. I read an article once about a man in Florida whose Airedale was devoured by an alligator right in front of his eyes. The man leaped heroically into the water and actually rode on the back of the alligator and beat it over the head trying to save his dog, but the big gator made off with the Airedale and that was the end of it. But this Airedale was swimming, not running.

TICKS

Ticks are capricious. In one brushy, grassy area there aren't any, and another place may be loaded. My dogs have seldom come back with ticks, but one day I picked twelve off Doc. Ticks are ugly to look at, but not hard to get rid of. If you think your dog may have been exposed to ticks, poke your fingers through his coat in the evening when you're home. Look especially carefully around the neck and behind the ears. If you find a tick, grasp it as close to the hide as you can and pull it slowly out. Don't worry about the head of the tick staying in the dog. It might bother you if that happened, because you have skin, but a dog has a hide, and there is no danger it will fester.

Foxtails can be a definite hazard for your dog whether he runs or not, but needn't be with a little alertness on your part. Foxtails are those dry, sharp parts of the grass that easily come off the plant and adhere to animals, people, and cloth in the early summer after the grass has turned brown and dry. Grass seed and many other fragments of plants can be equally dangerous. The problem occurs when these objects get between the dog's toes or inside the ears. A simple inspection of your dog will reveal if there is a problem. If your dog limps or shakes his head repeatedly, give him a careful inspection and remove the foxtail or other object if that is the problem. Sometimes surgical removal by your veterinarian is required.

OTHER DOGS

Dog fights are a bigger problem. Next to cars, I would say this is the worst problem you can have when you run with your dog. But remember, with rare exceptions, only male dogs fight. If you're worried about your dog getting into fights, run with a bitch. As I've mentioned, a bitch will seldom fight, and a male dog will practically never attack a bitch. Occasionally there's a bitch that will charge if she's approached too quickly by another dog, and if the other dog is touchy, there may be a problem. Also, some inexperienced male may act aggressively toward a female until he gets a good sniff, and if the female is the assertive type and won't back off, a fight could start. But even under these conditions, it's extremely unlikely it will become a serious matter, one of those "fight-to-the-death" struggles that males can get into. I've run with dogs and with bitches and I must confess it's more peaceful running with a bitch.

Sometimes the breed makes a difference, for certain breeds are more apt to fight than others. German Shepherds have a reputation for being fighters, but they vary widely from individual to individual, and many Alsatians wouldn't dream of wasting time fighting another dog. Dobermans, Rottweilers, and even German Shorthaired Pointers, because they are generally fearless animals, can also sometimes be fighters.

Pit Bull Terriers may also fight. After all, they're bred to do so, and they have the most powerful bite of any dog—twelve hundred pounds to the square inch. (German Shepherds are a distant second with eight hundred.) Pit Bulls can also be very friendly, however, and besides, you hardly ever run across one, especially when running. Any individual dog of any breed or mix, can turn out to be a fighter, but fortunately, with proper training, especially from puppyhood, this overly aggressive tendency can almost always be controlled. In extreme cases, the dog can be neutered, but personally I would consult a professional dog trainer before I did this. If your dog is overly aggressive toward human beings, especially toward children, destroying the dog is what must be done if a tragic incident is to be avoided.

Even if your male isn't a fighter and wouldn't think of starting a fight, the other male dog you meet might not be equally peace loving. There are a lot of things you can do to prevent dog fights, or break them up if they take place.

If your dog is running alongside you and another dog approaches, or you pass by a potentially dangerous dog, keep your dog close to you and keep moving away at a slow but steady pace. Sometimes it helps to carry a leash with you even though you don't use it all the time. If you have one, this may be a good time to use it to be sure your dog keeps close to you. It's a rare dog that will charge your dog when he's close by you, so this method usually does the trick.

If your dog and another male do meet, watch their behavior. They may give each other a cursory sniff and then run off to rejoin their masters. But they may also begin to walk stiffly around each other sniffing at each other's rear end. They are clearly psyching each other out. If the hair goes up on the back of their necks, they are beginning to trade insults. The

thing to do is not get excited and don't hang around. Keep on running slowly away, but turn your head back to your dog and call him to come. Clap your hands as you do so, so he gets the message loud and clear. Remember, male dogs usually fight to defend their territory, and out in the open they haven't established any territory so there's nothing for your dog to defend but you. If you aren't there because you're running on ahead, your dog will almost certainly exchange a final insult to his would-be adversary, and with male bravado trot off after you saying to the other dog as he departs, "I'd whip you good, but my master says I have to go."

The male of the species puts on a great aggressive show because he thinks it's his male duty, but most of the time he doesn't really want to have things get serious. I believe it was Konrad Lorenz (well-known specialist in animal behavior) who told the story of two dogs who lived next to each other, their yards divided by a fence with a locked gate. Back and forth they would race, each on a side of the fence. They barked and growled defiantly, apparently ready to tear each other apart. One day the gate was inadvertently left open and suddenly the two dogs were face to face with no fence between them! Disaster? Not at all. Both dogs simply turned and raced back along the fence growling and barking at each other again.

So the thing to do is keep your cool and see what happens. And whatever you do, don't hang around and get excited. This will only excite your dog, who may misinterpret your behavior to mean that he's supposed to fight. To prove he's not a coward, and to please you, he may then do so.

If a dog fight does start, remember that there is usually more noise than damage. Two dogs fighting sound dreadful; you are certain they are killing each other. But dogs have a loose hide, and a lot of hair, and it takes a while before a dog can penetrate all that and cause damage to the other. If your dog is fighting, follow the procedure described above and trot away, calling your dog. He probably doesn't want to fight and if things haven't gone too far he'll welcome the excuse to break it off with honor and run after you.

The real damage occurs when one dog gets a good grip on the other dog's throat. When this happens you may have to intervene. Effective procedures include throwing clothing over the head of the dominant dog, throwing sand or dirt in the dogs' faces, even using a weapon such as your shoes laced together so they can be swung at the dog from a short distance away. If you're near a hose, turn the water on them good and hard. One hopes the owner of the other dog will also be trying to help. The owner of the "top dog" may have to pry open the jaws of his dog. A stick may be necessary if the dog is especially strong. Some people carry high-frequency "screech alarms," because dogs don't like the sound and will break off the fighting to get away from it.

When Doc was getting to be an old dog, a much younger dog about his size insisted on approaching us when I was doing my preliminary exercises near the car. This time it really wasn't Doc's fault that the trouble started. He had done enough fighting in his youth and at his age he wasn't looking for trouble. But the other dog had an excitable master who lost his cool and began to yell and jump around and soon the fight started. I waited for the other owner to pull his dog off, but he couldn't get to him. I could see that Doc was trying not to fight, but the other dog was insistent. I could see it was getting serious, and because the other dog was younger and stronger, Doc was going to get the worst of it. I grabbed the other dog by his long tail and pulled him off. When the dog wheeled around to get at me, I just kept turning in a circle. It worked extremely well. It must have looked funny, but I felt safe, and finally the dog's owner corralled him to end the danger.

That's one way to break up a fight. The way not to break up one is to get between the dogs. You could get bitten yourself. Even your own dog might accidentally turn on you if he is really in a fighting fever.

To give your fighting dog credit, sometimes you have to admire him for it. One day my wife, small son, and I, together with Doc, were visiting a friend in the mountains. He had a nifty little cabin up a rough dirt road. It was winter and the road was so muddy we couldn't drive up it. We had to walk any time we wanted to go to the cabin or to the car. This took us past another cabin where three tough looking young men were living with their three fierce-looking Newfoundlands. My friend warned me that the three young men and their dogs were all nasty characters with a bad reputation. The men had already been warned by the authorities about their dogs that they just let run loose.

As luck would have it, as we were returning to our cabin, they all were outside, not far from the road—the three young men and their three Newfoundlands, huge, black animals, weighing at least 150 pounds each. The worst looking one of all was right by the side of the road. We stopped. I held Doc, and we politely asked the young men to hold their dogs while we passed by. They just looked at us coldly. We waited a bit, not quite knowing what to do. The dogs moved closer. Suddenly the worst looking Newfoundland lunged toward us. Quick as a flash, Doc broke free of me and sailed into the Newfoundland, even though his opponent weighed over twice as much as he did. "Oh no," I thought,

"this is it. My dog will start to get killed and then I'll have to go in and try to save him and then I'll get killed." The fight was really a bad one; it looked as though the dogs really meant it. I moved in reluctantly to do something, since the owners of the Newfoundland were just standing back enjoying the spectacle. How those dogs were going at it! Growling and tearing at each other. And then, suddenly, that Newfoundland broke and ran back to his cabin! And with that, the other two Newfoundlands that were hovering nearby also took flight. Doc stood triumphantly claiming the field. He was proud of himself for having successfully defended his family. Evidently chagrined, the young men disappeared inside their cabin without a word. Truly it is said that a bully, when beaten, turns craven.

I learned some months later from my friend that the police arrested all three of the young men for dealing with drugs and confiscated the dogs.

By the way, there's no slur against the character of Newfoundlands intended in this story. Newfoundlands are great animals, but most dogs take on the characteristics of their owners. I believe that the men who owned these three were aggressive and cruel but cowards at heart, just like their dogs.

If there has been a fight, examine your dog carefully, even if you don't think he is injured. Look for small puncture wounds that may not be obvious but could cause trouble later through infection. A dog's eyes, nose, ears, and face are especially vulnerable. If there is any sign of blood, it won't hurt to call your vet and ask his advice. If no vet is available or if you have to use first aid, put some neosporin on the wound.

Some people get pretty uptight about letting dogs run free under any circumstances. I can hear these people saying, "Well, if only people would keep their dogs on a leash where they belong there wouldn't be any trouble." The fact is that the worst dog fight I ever heard of that involved a runner and his dog occurred in a nice neighborhood with a carefully leashed dog. My friend was running through an ordinary suburban area with his dog on a leash when a German Shepherd rushed out of a house and with no warning threw himself on my friend's dog and got a fierce hold on his throat. The owner of the attacking dog came right after his animal, but it was hard to break the Shepherd's grip. My friend finally made the dog let go, but the price he paid was a badly torn hand that had to be treated at the hospital. He was extremely lucky that the Shepherd's teeth didn't tear vital ligaments in his hand but only made flesh wounds.

The fact is, you're in more danger of dog fights walking around the neighborhood with your dog on a leash than out in open country with your dog running free. The German Shepherd evidently regarded the sidewalk in front of his house as part of his territory to be defended against an intruder. It's because of the territorial instinct that the friendly neighborhood may not be so friendly after all, and your dog's leash may only make it harder for him to defend himself. Even the dog fight between Doc and the young dog took place around cars; no doubt the attacking dog believed he had a solemn duty to drive Doc away from his master's car. In San Clemente Canyon and Fiesta Island, on the other hand, I've had threatening situations, but never an actual fight.

For this reason, if you're planning to run or walk your dog in an unfamiliar neighborhood, it may be a good idea to first case it out to see if there are aggressive dogs, and if so, where they are. If you locate one, run or walk with your dog on the other side of the street; the aggressive dog may bark when you come by, but it's unlikely he'll attack since you are not on his territory.

Cuts

Another potential danger if you hike, hunt, or run with your dog in the woods or back country is cuts. The sad fact is that those nice clean woods may conceal old barbed wire, boards with protruding nails, broken glass, sharp pieces of old metal containers, or even traps set out for wild animals, and your dog could get cut from any of these objects. If your dog is bleeding, the first task will be to stop the bleeding. If the bleeding is rapid, comes in spurts, or is bright red in color, an artery may be severed. Try controlling the bleeding by direct pressure over the wound. If this does not work, apply a tourniquet. Tighten the tourniquet until the bleeding stops, but be sure to release it every fifteen minutes for a short while to let the blood circulate. If the bleeding is slower, it is only a vein that is severed and a bandage over the wound should stop it. Be sure to give your dog plenty of water—dehydration from bleeding can be a severe problem. And, of course, give up your hunt or hike or run and get the dog to your veterinarian at once. Watch the animal closely for signs of shock, which may include a slow pulse, sharp increase in respiration rate, and pale gums. Keep the animal warm if the day is cool.

By now you may be so frightened by these possible hazards of running with your dog that you may vow never to do so. But don't be frightened. If you don't want to take chances, run with a spayed bitch in a place where there are no snakes and no cars. It will be pleasure all the way. Regardless of where you run, if you use your head there is not likely to be any difficulty. As I've said, I've run with a lot of different dogs for twenty years and seldom had a problem. My great dog Doc died at the age of thirteen without ever having had a sick day in his life until his advanced old age. I'm convinced Doc would have had more problems if he hadn't run. Besides, your dog's not as safe in the backyard as you think. He can get sick from sprays on plants, can choke on the backyard tennis ball, and can be injured by rushing into the street on that inevitable occasion when he finds the gate open and out of sheer relief from boredom and inexperience dashes in front of a car.

You have to have a philosophy about it. Is it better to confine your dog to a backyard life and have it die from boredom or some disease, or is it better to let your dog run even though you have to take a few chances? It's the same with children. They grow up and have to cross streets by themselves; they learn to drive cars and you have to turn them loose on the freeways. They could get hurt, and sometimes they do. But you can't lock up a living creature and throw away the key because you're afraid of injury. If you did, it wouldn't help, for everything that is alive has to do its thing in life or suffer a spiritual malaise that may bring on illness and early death. So let your dog run with you. Chances are there will be no problems. Even if your dog should get hurt, at least he has really been living. If you ask your dog which way he wants it—the safe backyard existence or a life with some adventure—you can be sure he will say, "Let's go running!"

Running and Your Dog's Health

To have a healthy dog you get a strong puppy from a healthy litter. Most dogs are tough, strong animals, although over-breeding has turned some once fine breeds into caricatures of what they were originally meant to be. Irish Setters are an example. These dogs were once robust hunting dogs. Their beautiful red coats, however, made them too popular and, in satisfying the demand, careless breeders produced some strains of nervous, unstable animals. Happily for Irish Setter lovers, there are still a number of sturdy specimens around.

Sometimes irresponsible breeding has perpetuated problems when careful breeding might have eliminated the difficulty. Take German Shepherds. To meet the popular demand for a guard dog, thoughtless breeding produced too many of these dogs with hip dysplasia. Another theory has it that this trait was originally bred into the dog to satisfy dog show judges who favored the German Shepherd's low, crouching gait. For whatever reason, it's unfortunate that such a truly great dog as the German Shepherd should be damaged in this way. There are still a number of healthy Alsatians around, and a goodly number of responsible breeders trying to produce a strain of German Shepherds free of this problem.

If fact, there are enough responsible breeders of German Shepherds who are alert to the problem of hip dysplasia that other large breeds of dogs are turning up with the problem as often as, or more often than, the Alsatians. Hip dysplasia is now reported in many large dogs such as Golden Retrievers, Siberian Huskies, Saint Bernards, Great Danes, Old English Sheepdogs, Rottweilers, Akitas, and Collies, and even in some smaller dogs such as Cockers and Shelties. A good breeder will not breed a dog that has undesirable characteristics, but a careless breeder will. An overzealous, uninformed backyard breeder may also create the problem unwittingly by overfeeding the puppies. If you have a litter of pups in your backyard and aren't sure how to proceed, consult your vet or a professional dog breeder.

So when you select a breed of dog, especially if you want the dog to run with you, you may wish to choose a dog that isn't quite as popular and thereby avoid the problems that come from careless breeding of the more popular dogs. A good choice might be an Airedale, or a dog with a well-deserved reputation for good health and disposition, such as a Labrador Retriever. Better yet, know your breeder and buy from one with a good reputation. Or, you may want a mongrel, a dog that has many different strains in him; or a mix, one whose father was one breed and mother another. If you choose a mix, try to get one that combines two dogs of the same general type so that the dog's instincts are not confused. For instance, a dog that is a cross between two hunting types of dogs (a Lab and a Pointer) or two working types of dogs (a German Shepherd and a Collie). A mix-breed may not win you medals in a dog show, but is likely to be relatively free of congenital defects, and a happy, sturdy family dog.

The individual animal you choose, as well as the breeder, will be as important as the breed you select. For example, a dog that is to be bonded to human beings will need warm, human contact during the first twelve weeks of its life. If you choose a puppy from people who are only breeding dogs for money and have not given the puppies care and love, your dog may never mature socially. If your dog comes from a retail pet store where the pups are left alone in a show window without human contact, the same problem may develop. It isn't hard to select a good puppy, but there are important things to know. A good guide is Peter J. Vollmer's pamphlet "Puppy Rearing." The bibliography advises you where to obtain this pamphlet.

Regardless of what kind of dog you have, it will be your job as his owner to observe your animal carefully. If you decide to run him, you will need to watch him extra closely to learn how much he can take.

Chances are your dog will be able to take more than you can, except for the heat. Dogs don't handle heat very well. Nature bred them mostly for cold weather. Their furry coats are great for the cold, but ill adapted for running in the summer in Georgia or Arizona. And some breeds, such as Labradors and Chesapeake Bay Retrievers, in addition to their fur coats, have a layer of cold-insulating fat underneath their hide, a lot like the blubber that keeps whales and seals warm in the icy waters of the Arctic.

To make it more complicated, a dog's cooling mechanism isn't as efficient as that of a human being, who can cool down by sweating. A dog only sweats through the pads of his feet. His only real way to cool down his body temperature is by panting, and this isn't as good as an effective perspiration system. How would you get along running in eighty-degree heat wearing a fur coat and not being able to perspire? That's roughly the situation a dog is up against.

If your dog gets too hot, heat exhaustion can set in. Heat exhaustion is a rise in body temperature sufficient to cause physical damage to the tissues. If you are running on a warm day and see your dog slow down, begin to tire, and get a glazed look in his eyes, suspect heat exhaustion and stop running immediately. If he has bright red or bleeding gums, shows signs of weakness or stupor, or should stagger or go into convulsions, you can be almost sure of it. Do what you would do for a human being in similar circumstances—stop the dog from running, get him into the shade, and cool him down with water if it is available. If the symptoms persist or have been extreme—staggering, bleeding, or convulsions—take your dog to your vet, even if he seems to have recovered. There is a chance of damage to his liver or kidneys.

Don't be too reluctant to take your dog with you on a warm day. Let him go on the shorter runs instead of the long ones. If he is a long-haired dog, get him a summer haircut. Try to run in cooler places, near the ocean or in a shaded area. Choose a cooler time of day. If it's going to be a long run, make sure there is drinking water available, even when it means taking water along in the car and planning the run so you return to the car occasionally. Best of all, run near a body of water if you can, so the dog can take a quick plunge when he needs to cool down. He'll really enjoy that and it will do the job. If you follow these procedures, you can safely run with your dog in summer. Your dog will enjoy the summer a lot more than if he spends it all in the backyard.

What if it's cold? Great! Dogs love it cold. It can hardly get too cold for them. You may have to bundle up, but your dog will charge about happily even when the temperature is freezing or less, if he was bred for nothern climates. Remember, however, to take precautions if you have a small, short-haired dog. On long runs, your dog could lose too much body heat. The larger the dog the more resistant he will be to body heat loss. If you have reason to suspect that your small dog may be exposed to too much low temperature, a dog sweater will help.

All runners, including people *and* dogs, need good nutrition. Most regular runners take care to eat well, and many take vitamin and mineral supplements. They do this because running burns up a lot of energy and many nutrients. Our running dog also needs a good, well-balanced diet, and most dry dog food preparations will give that to your dog. In these days when commercial, processed foods are under criticism for their poor nutrition, it's good to know that the opposite is true with dry dog foods. Veterinarian and columnist Anna P. Clarke, in answer to a question about how to prepare a good diet for a dog, replied:

> Most veterinarians recommend that dog owners take
> advantage of the wealth of scientific knowledge available
> and feed their dogs the specially formulated and
> guaranteed completely balanced dog foods.*

Canned dog food, on the other hand, isn't usually as good as dry food in supplying a balanced diet. It's nutritionally inferior to the dry food, is

*(Parade Magazine, October 1982.)

expensive, and is mostly water anyhow. "People food," such as your table scraps, will be popular with your dog, but scraps are no better for him than his regular food, and will certainly spoil him for dog food. Try never giving him anything but a good commercial dog food. As long as he doesn't know there is anything that tastes better, he'll be entirely satisfied and just as healthy. Your vet may recommend supplements to help keep him that way.

Meanwhile, the good exercise you are giving your dog will help keep him lean and free of the negative effects of obesity. Veterinarians say that excess weight decreases the animal's health and increases its tendency toward disease. The extra weight taxes the heart by requiring extra blood. Other disorders, such as kidney problems, hip dysplasia, pancreatitis, and diabetes, are also aggravated by obesity.

Of course, a dog can get too thin. A good rule of thumb is to keep your dog's weight low enough so you can feel his ribs with your hand, and high enough so the ribs don't stick out through his hide. He should be well muscled, with a smooth chest and well-formed legs. If he is kept lean and strong, he will be physically and psychologically better off. A combination of right nutrition and proper exercise is the way to keep dogs, and people, healthy.

When dogs run they sometimes injure themselves, just as people can do. You have to keep an eye out for this possibility. Fortunately, most injuries are obvious. They include things like stiffness, temporary depletion of bodily resources, and injuries to a paw, such as soreness, cuts, or an imbedded foreign object. As far as I know, dogs practically never get the injuries common among human runners, such as tendinitis, knee injuries, or stress fractures.

The paw is the most vulnerable part of a running dog's body. If the dog is favoring one paw, something is obviously wrong and a simple inspection usually reveals the difficulty. If it's a cut, you can probably see it; when in doubt use a magnifying glass to make sure you haven't overlooked a minor injury. Look closely to see if there is a small thorn or other sharp object. If the dog's paws are sore, it may be because you are running on too hard a surface—such as asphalt, concrete, or ice. A dog's paw wasn't designed for that, but even so, once the dog is toughened up he should be able to run almost anywhere.

Don't panic when your dog's paw is injured. Nature knows the paw is likely to get hurt and has seen to it that cuts and other such injuries heal with astonishing rapidity. Let the dog rest and heal before you put him under more stress. Visit your vet if the paw doesn't seem to be improving properly.

When your dog becomes stiff from a long run, it's probably just because you ran hard. You'll probably be a little stiff too. But if it happens often, or the dog shows signs of pain, he could have some arthritis. This common human ailment shows up in many animals. If you suspect arthritis, see your vet.

If you run hard one day, you'll want to take it easy the next day to allow your body, and your dog's, to renew itself. If you don't rest, you'll feel flat when you run, and will be more prone to injury. Your dog's body has a similar need. When he seems reluctant to run, let him have a day off. His body is telling him he needs it. If the malaise continues, however, and especially if he refuses food, you have to consider the possibility that your dog is ill.

I've pointed out the injuries your dog may incur while running. They are few and far between. The fact is, as I have mentioned before, a running dog is a healthier dog, other things being equal. A well-nourished, loved, and properly exercised dog will be much more disease resistant than a pampered stay-at-home pooch. I have no statistics to back that up because there aren't any available that I know of, but I have lots of experience. After running with a variety of dogs all these years, I have yet to have any of them spend one single day being sick. Injuries occasionally—sickness never. No infectious diseases. No heart problems. Of course I regularly took the dogs to the vet for inoculations and a look-over, and they had a secure and predictable home environment with lots of love from members of the family. Running is no substitute for the other necessities of life, but with dogs, as with people, exercise and health tend to go together.

I must mention one other benefit that exercise will bring to your dog: he'll look so good that you'll be proud of him. If you run your dog, he'll have the look about him that a sedentary dog can't have. A running dog will be sleek with a well-developed muscular structure and strong-looking chest. He will also have a certain bearing about him that I call confidence. It will be there in your dog and he'll hold himself just a little differently from the way other dogs do. Don't be surprised if neighbors or people you meet while running make an admiring comment about your animal. And, if you should like to show your dog, don't be surprised if your dog's exercise program influences the judges in his favor. All of this, of course, will make you proud of your dog, and don't think your dog doesn't know it! Like children, dogs know just how we feel about them, and that influences how they feel about themselves.

We have noted that it's generally easier to run with a bitch than with a dog. One exception is when the bitch goes into heat. When your bitch is in heat, leave her home! If you don't, she'll attract every male dog within two miles, and even the best behaved dog goes crazy when there's a bitch in heat around. That's Mother Nature's very effective way of guaranteeing that the canine species doesn't perish. Do yourself, your bitch, and everyone else a favor by letting her stay quietly at home, or, better yet, in a kennel, until her heat is over. She may not mind. Like the females of many species, her heat is a time when she becomes quieter and more reflective than usual, until the male dog shows up!

How about running your dog with a bike? I've done it, so it can work. Since you go faster on a bike than when you're running, your dog needs to be strong and fast. It can be a great way to exercise your dog, except that you will probably have to run your dog on a road where there are cars. You may have to train him to run alongside the bike on a leash without pulling suddenly to the side, which could be dangerous for you. The training process shouldn't be too difficult if you are willing to try it. Your dog will certainly enjoy running beside your bike.

I must confess that I ran into one problem running a dog with a bike that I never did solve. I've mentioned the Doberman Pinscher that lived with me for a year. He was a great running dog, strong and fast, easily able to keep up with me on a bike. But he got it into his head that it was a game and insisted on biting at the bike's front wheel. I never did figure a way to train the dog out of it and finally had to give up biking with him.

Don't despair when you have a problem running with your dog. There's almost always a way to correct it. Since my difficulty with the Doberman, people have given me creative suggestions. One is to train the dog to run alongside the bike on a leash first; this way he'll learn the proper position to take. A second suggestion is to carry an atomizer with you and when he runs in front of the bike or bites the wheel, let him have it with a harmless liquid.

If running your dog with a bike is good, then running him with a car is better—right? Maybe. An obvious problem is that when you run your dog with a car, you won't get any exercise. There are times when you *don't* want exercise, say you've been sick, and you would welcome a chance to give your dog a quick, strenuous run without having to exert yourself. If you can find the proper place where it's safe for the dog, running him with the car may be the answer.

Many people think this is terribly cruel. My own family used to object strongly when I occasionally had to resort to running the Doberman and my mix-breed Doc with the car. They gave me horrified looks when I told them what I had done, and spoke to me as though I was some kind of monster. However, I've watched lots of dogs being run behind cars on San Diego's Fiesta Island and the dogs look to me as though they are enjoying it hugely. They know they aren't going to be left behind. It's a game to them, like chasing rabbits. Naturally, you'll want your dog running behind the car only if your dog is young, strong, and healthy. It would be cruel to run your dog this way if he wasn't up to it.

The mention of cars brings up a few more points. Dogs make a mess out of cars, especially running dogs. They come back from the run panting, dripping wet, muddy, and sandy. They love it, but you won't love them when they climb into the back seat of your favorite Cadillac. If you can, try to keep an old car around that you don't care about. I have an ancient station wagon with well over 100,000 miles on it. The dirtier it gets, the more character it has. It has carried so many happy, wet dogs that it thinks that's what it was designed for. It doesn't matter to me how dirty this car gets, and it doesn't matter if I leave it in some out-of-the-way places while my dog and I go do our thing because no one would want to steal it.

If you have a pickup truck, you can stick the dog in the back of the truck. The back can get dirty and the front, where you sit with your wife or girl friend, can stay clean and pretty. But is it safe for a dog to ride in the back of a truck? I die a thousand deaths watching a dog sitting in the back of a truck hurtling along a freeway at sixty miles per hour. I figure there must be some special guardian angel who keeps the dog from falling out. The truth is that dogs do fall out sometimes. If you have to make a sudden maneuver or have an accident, you could have a bad problem. So if you want to carry your dog in an uncovered pickup truck, you're taking a chance. To be safe, however, you could buy a suitably sized airline shipping crate, fasten it securely to the bed of the truck, and carry your dog in that. The crates come in five sizes, so no matter the size of your dog, there's a crate that will fit him. This will keep him from jumping out and protect him from being slammed around and from flying debris. It will cost you a little money, but less than a big bill from a vet to fix a broken leg. Better yet is to buy a camper shell to put on the back of your truck so your dog can't jump out and he will also have shelter.

Just as you want to keep your Cadillac clean by leaving it behind when you take your dog running, you'll also want to keep your wife or husband happy by leaving your wet, muddy, four-footed friend in the backyard until he can come into the house as a clean, respectable member of the family. She or he probably loves your dog as much as you do, but you both will be loved a lot more if you keep the dog outside until he's clean. It won't be long. Dogs dry off fast, and their coats become clean and slick again. A few strokes with the brush will be all that's necessary to have a clean, dry dog ready to sit contentedly by the family fire at night. And you'll have a happy household to boot.

Some people have more than one dog; I have at times. There is no reason not to run them both, but remember that one dog often gets the other dog stirred up. If you add one enthusiastic dog to the company of another enthusiastic dog, you get two very enthusiastic dogs that can generate surprising amounts of energy. It's lots of fun to watch, but it may take more energy out of you to keep track of them, making sure they are safe and not bothering anyone.

One dog is company for you, two dogs are company for each other, but three or more dogs make up a pack. That means when you get three or more dogs together, their behavior changes. Dogs that form packs can become feral dogs, which are domestic dogs that have become wild. They are less controllable and more dangerous than canids in the wild, perhaps because they have the wildness of their free-running cousins without their controlling instincts and fear of man. Feral packs have been known to tyrannize neighborhoods and to go on rampages at night destroying wildstock. Many losses blamed on coyotes may be caused by feral dogs. I don't mean to imply that you shouldn't own or run with more than one dog, but to point out that you might run into unusual behavior problems if you do.

It's not all bad, however, to have several dogs. A friend told me of a time when she was walking with her four Shelties. Two big Dobermans approached them aggressively. The four Shelties rushed at the Dobies and put up such a fierce, courageous display that the bigger dogs departed hurriedly. She added that the Shelties acted as if they were enjoying it. If nothing else, having a dog pack with you gives you a lot of protection.

One last special situation that I briefly touched on in the second chapter is that some runners like to run in races. You may have your favorite races—ten-kilometer races or even marathons. Should you let your dog run with you in the race? Some races permit it, or at least they haven't thought of a rule against it. I've run in races in which an owner ran with his dog on a leash and people seemed to enjoy it. Dog, owner, and everyone who passed by seemed to feel it added to the joy and freedom of the occasion. However, I read an article by someone objecting to dogs racing with their owners, claiming the dog cut in front of some runners and generally caused problems. Maybe so. If your dog causes other runners problems, you'll have to leave him home when you race. There are also some people who don't like dogs, not because dogs cause problems, but because they just don't like them. Maybe they think dogs ought to be like people, and can't understand why they act like animals instead. Even if you feel the objection to your race-running dog isn't fair, you'll still probably want to leave him home. No need to expose your properly trained, gentlemanly, four-footed friend to such unpleasant characters. He deserves good company, just as you do.

So there it is. No one will ever know how or why people and canids began running together. Whoever they were, they started a great tradition. When you run with your dog, some part deep inside you will hark back to that primitive man and primeval dog who ran together over the African Veldt or through an ancient European forest. The thud of your feet on the ground will echo through your soul and reawaken ancient memories. When you and your dog run together, you won't be alone—that first man and dog team will be running with you. They'll be glad, and so will you. To you and your dog—happy running!

Bibliography

Boone, J. Allen. *Kinship With All Life*. New York: Harper and Row, 1954.

Fixx, James F. *The Complete Book of Running*. New York: Random House, 1977.

Fox, Michael W. *Soul of the Wolf*. Boston: Little, Brown & Co. 1980.

Gray, Robert. *The Natural Life of North American Wolves*. New York: W. W. Norton & Co., Inc., 1970.

Hurrell, James, DVM. *Running With Your Dog*. Drayton Plains Veterinarian Hospital 3980 Walton Blvd., Drayton Plains, Michigan 48020, 1981 (pamphlet).

Kalstone, Shirlee and McNamara, Walter. *First Aid for Dogs*. Bantam Books, 1983.

Kipling, Rudyard. *The Jungle Book*.

Leslie, Robert F. *In the Shadow of a Rainbow, The True Story of a Friendship Between Man and Wolf*. New York: W. W. Norton & Co., Inc. 1974.

Lorenz, Konrad. *Man Meets Dog*. New York: Penguin Books, Inc., 1965.

Mowat, Farley. *Never Cry Wolf*. Boston: Little, Brown & Co., 1963.

Nabokov, Peter. *Indian Running*. Santa Barbara, California: Capra Press, 1981.

Pringle, Laurence. *The Controversial Coyote, Predation, Politics, and Ecology*. New York: Harcourt, Brace, Jovanovich, 1977.

Ryden, Hope. *God's Dog, A Celebration of the North American Coyote*. New York: The Viking Press, 1975.

Seton, Ernest Thompson. *Wild Animals I Have Known*. New York: Charles Scribner's Sons, 1898, 1926.

Subotnick, Steven I. *Cures for Common Running Injuries*. Mountain View, California: Anderson World, Inc., 1979.

Vollmer, Peter J. *Puppy Rearing, Guidelines on Bringing Up a Dog*. Hill's Pet Products, P.O. Box 148, Topeka, Kansas 66601, 1978 (pamphlet).

Woodhouse, Barbara. *No Bad Dogs The Woodhouse Way*. New York: Summit Books, 1978.